THE DEACON AT MASS

Other Paulist Press Books
By, For, and About Deacons

Deacons and the Church
by Owen F. Cummings

101 Questions and Answers on Deacons
by William T. Ditewig

Theology of the Diaconate: The State of the Question
by Owen F. Cummings,
William T. Ditewig, and Richard Gaillardetz

Saintly Deacons
by Owen F. Cummings

Preach What You Believe: Timeless Homilies
for Deacons—Liturgical Cycle B
by Michael E. Bulson

Believe What You Read: Timeless Homilies
for Deacons—Liturgical Cycle C
by Michael E. Bulson

The Deacon Reader: New Issues and Cross-Currents
edited by James Keating

Today's Deacon: Contemporary Issues and Cross-Currents
by Alfred C. Hughes, Frederick F. Campbell,
and William T. Ditewig

The Permanent Diaconate: Its History and
Place in the Sacrament of Orders
by Kenan Osborne, OFM

The Emerging Diaconate
by William T. Ditewig

THE DEACON AT MASS

A Theological and Pastoral Guide

William T. Ditewig

Paulist Press
New York/Mahwah, NJ

Cover design by Joy Taylor
Book design by Lynn Else

Library of Congress Cataloging-in-Publication Data

Ditewig, William T.
    The deacon at mass : a theological and pastoral guide / William T. Ditewig.
    p. cm.
    Includes bibliographical references.
    ISBN 978–0–8091–4465–5 (alk. paper)
    1. Deacons—Catholic Church. 2. Mass I. Title.
    BX1913.D375 2007
    264′.0203—dc22

                                                    2006035340

Published by Paulist Press
997 Macarthur Boulevard
Mahwah, New Jersey 07430

www.paulistpress.com

Printed and bound in the United States of America

For my mother, Kathleen,

Who first taught me the Latin of the
Mass so I could be an altar server;

For the priests and School Sisters of Notre Dame
at St. Patrick Parish, who first introduced
me to the wonders of liturgy;

For our loving family,
Who gives meaning to everything.

Religion that is pure and undefiled before
God, the Father, is this:
to care for orphans and widows in their distress,
and to keep oneself unstained by the world.
—Letter of James 1:27

Contents

Foreword by *Catherine Dooley, OP, PhD* ix

Acknowledgments xi

Prayer for Deacons..xiii

Introduction: Contemporary Deacons and the Eucharist......1
   The Renewed Diaconate: Why?....................................3
   The Dangers of Functionalism..................................7
   The Deacon's and the Bishop's Ministries 8
   The Eucharist as "Source and Summit" of the
      Deacon's Ministry and Life 13
   The Deacon and the New GIRM 16
   Conclusions...19

Chapter One: Preparation and Planning..........................21
   Principles and Commentary 21
      The Role of the Deacon at Mass 21
      The Deacon and the Elements of the Mass................27
      Vestments 34
   Conclusions...38
   Questions for Reflection and Future Planning..............40

Chapter Two: Introductory Rites 41
   Principles and Commentary 41
      Text of the GIRM on the Introductory Rites...........41
      Commentary...45

Contents

Conclusions...50

Questions for Reflection and Future Planning..............51

Chapter Three: Liturgy of the Word 52

Principles and Commentary 52

Text of the GIRM on the Liturgy of the Word.........52

Commentary...57

Conclusions...66

Questions for Reflection and Future Planning..............67

Chapter Four: Liturgy of the Eucharist 68

Principles and Commentary 68

Text of the GIRM on the Liturgy of the Eucharist ...68

Commentary...74

Conclusions...84

Questions for Reflection and Future Planning..............85

Chapter Five: Concluding Rites....................................86

Principles and Commentary 86

Text of the GIRM on the Concluding Rites..............86

Commentary...87

Questions for Reflection and Future Planning..............89

**Concluding Reflection: The Deacon in the
Sacred Liturgy** 90

Appendix: Liturgical Vestments of the Deacon.................93

Glossary 96

Bibliography..99

Foreword

The ancient axiom *lex orandi, lex credendi* (the law of prayer establishes the law of belief) is at the heart of this book. *The Deacon at Mass: A Theological and Pastoral Guide* is a practical resource for deacons, priests, and all who mentor and support the ministry of the deacon, especially at the Liturgy of the Eucharist of the Latin Rite of the Catholic Church. Deacon Ditewig's breadth of knowledge of the teachings of Vatican II and its subsequent documents provides a trove of primary references on the liturgical ministry of the deacon and all who are dedicated to the restoration of the permanence of the diaconate. The guide offers many practical suggestions for celebrating the liturgy, but it is not simply a "how-to" for the deacon. Its primary focus is to provide a solid theological commentary on the spiritual dimension of the ritual actions. All of this is placed within the context of the vocation of the deacon whose ministry is meant to be Word, sacrament, and servant-leadership.

Celebrating the Eucharist well is the aim of the book. If liturgy is to be celebrated well, the formation of the liturgical ministers is a requisite. The Constitution on the Sacred Liturgy *(Sacrosanctum Concilium)* states that the purpose of the liturgy is primarily worship but that it also instructs (no. 33). The Constitution over and over again calls for a formation that promotes a full, active, and conscious participation of all the people. It calls for a catechesis that includes appropriation of the foundational documents on the liturgy in order to internalize the theology and pastoral principles that underlie this vision. It also suggests that the theology and structure of the rite be the foundation of the catechesis so that that liturgy itself "teaches."

Liturgical formation depends upon a strong and vital liturgy. When the community comes together in public worship, the ritual not only unites participants but is a means of transformation. Liturgy shapes the way we think and act because it sets out a vision of the reign of God. "Good celebrations foster and nourish faith. Poor celebrations may weaken and destroy it."* In this guide Dr. Ditewig has made a significant contribution to the liturgical catechesis of deacons and ultimately to all of us by offering a vision of the Liturgy of the Eucharist that is faithful to the tradition of the church and one that calls us to full, active participation in the saving act of Christ.

Catherine Dooley, OP, PhD
School of Theology and Religious Studies
The Catholic University of America

---

*Bishops' Committee on Liturgy, *Music in Catholic Worship* (Washington, DC: National Conference of Catholic Bishops, 1982), #6.

Acknowledgments

It is both truism and truth to observe that no published work is ever the work of a single person. Inspiration, encouragement, critical evaluation, and motivation all contribute to the process, and all come from a variety of sources.

In this case, I want to acknowledge Mr. Kevin Carrizo di Camillo, editor par excellence at Paulist Press. It was Kevin who several years ago first encouraged what has developed into a series of materials by, for, and about deacons through Paulist Press. He has been a constant champion of all of these projects and has guided them skillfully through the publishing process. Acknowledgment is also offered to Paulist Press publisher and president, Rev. Lawrence Boadt, CSP; managing editor, Mr. Paul McMahon; and the rest of the team at Paulist Press for their enthusiastic support of the diaconate.

I also need to acknowledge the support of my friends and mentors at the Catholic University of America and St. Mary-of-the-Woods College, especially Drs. Kate Dooley, OP, and Joseph A. Komonchak of CUA, and Drs. Ruth Eileen Dwyer, SP, and Alexa Suezer, SP, of SMWC. Not only have these "teachers-become-friends" offered encouragement over the years, they have become models of scholarship, faithfulness, and spirituality, which I can only hope to emulate.

Over the past decade, often in conjunction with the preparation and implementation of the *National Directory for the Formation, Ministry, and Life of Permanent Deacons in the United States,* it has been a great blessing to visit many dioceses here in the United States and around the world to support the renewal of the diaconate. Many of the insights and observations contained in this book are the result of conversations, complaints, questions, and concerns shared by deacons, priests, bishops, and laity. There is something quite special about the diaconate community (which consists of many more than just deacons); in many ways, the diaconate community is a coauthor of this book.

And how can one adequately acknowledge the contributions of one's own family? Our children, and now our grandchildren, have known for years of Dad's and Grandpa's constant tap-tap-tapping on the keyboard on some project or other. And my wife, Diann, accomplished artist as well as wife, mother, and grandmother, is herself a master of multitasking and has always been there to keep us on track and inspired to go on.

And so, from the bottom of my heart, my heartfelt love, thanks, and appreciation.

Prayer for Deacons

We praise you Father, Creator of all things,
Who teaches us how to love and
Who guides us on our journey of service.

Have mercy on us, forgive us our failings, and
Show us the way to be faithful servants.

We thank You for our families and
The faith communities who support us,
And we ask You to bless and watch over them.

Give us the grace to open our minds and hearts as we
Grow in wisdom, faith, and love of You and Your Word.

Send down Your Spirit, Lord,
To sustain us as we accept Your call to be
Heralds of Your Word, servants at Your Table, and
Ministers of charity to Your people.

With the intercession of
Blessed Mary, Mother of God,
St. John the Baptist, who inspires us to be Your voice,
And all Your saintly deacons,
We pray in the name of Jesus, our Lord and Savior,
In union with the Holy Spirit.
Amen.

Composed by Deacon Candidates
of the Diocese of Springfield in Massachusetts

INTRODUCTION

Contemporary Deacons and the Eucharist

———————

It is important at the outset to sketch the parameters of this guide. As the name implies, this book is meant to be a practical resource on the liturgical ministry of the deacon, especially at the Liturgy of the Eucharist of the Latin Rite of the Catholic Church (most often called Holy Mass or, simply, the Mass). It is intended for deacons and priests, candidates for ordination, and both parish and diocesan liturgical planners. However, this is more than a simple user's manual to follow when a deacon exercises liturgical ministry at Mass. While many of the technical details of this part of the deacon's ministry are provided, the focus of the book is to provide a theological and pastoral framework within which the deacon's liturgical role occurs.

It is extremely important to understand the theological context within which the deacons' liturgical ministry takes place. In practical terms, we might say that while it is important to know *what* a deacon does at Mass, it is even more important to understand *why* the deacon does it. Where are we to situate the deacon's liturgical and sacramental ministry within the full range of the diaconal ministry for which he has been ordained? This introduction briefly outlines several points that should be kept in mind when considering the liturgical ministry of the deacon.

Before proceeding further, two important disclaimers must be made. First, this book will not treat the liturgical ministry of deacons of the Eastern Catholic Churches. While much of the theological background offered in this book will have relevance for the East due to the centrality of the Eucharistic Mystery for all of us, the technical dimensions and the rich theological depths of the Eastern traditions demand a proper, substantive treatment of their own with regard to the participation of the deacon. The work of Chorbishop Seely Beggiani, Hans-Joachim Schulz, and others offers valuable insights, and on a popular level, Deacon Ed Faulk provides a good review of many dimensions of the Eastern deacon's liturgical role.[1]

The second disclaimer pertains to the limiting of this book to the deacon's role at Mass, when he has many other sacramental and liturgical roles as well. The most fundamental reason for focusing on the Mass is the fundamental character of the Mass itself. The classic statement from the Second Vatican Council that the Eucharistic Liturgy is "the

---

1. For example, Seely Beggiani, *The Divine Liturgy of the Maronite Church (History and Commentary)* (Glen Allen, VA: St. Maron Publications, 1998); Hans-Joachim Schulz, *The Byzantine Liturgy: Symbolic Structure and Faith Expression,* trans. Matthew J. O'Connell (New York: Pueblo Publishing Company, 1986); Ed Faulk, *101 Questions and Answers on the Eastern Catholic Churches* (Mahwah, NJ: Paulist Press, 2007).

summit toward which the activity of the church is directed, and at the same time it is the font from which all her strength flows"[2] suggests a freestanding treatment. On a practical level, the promulgation in 2000 of the Third Typical Edition of the *Roman Missal,* and its related *General Instruction of the Roman Missal* (GIRM) in 2002, demands renewed and focused attention on the deacon's role at Mass as described within these documents.

The Renewed Diaconate: Why?

Many people realize that the diaconate was renewed by the Second Vatican Council (1962–65) as a *permanent* part of ordained ministry, but fewer people understand *why* the council took this step. In order to avoid misunderstanding and confusion, it is important to grasp some of the reasons that led the world's bishops to restore the *permanence* of the diaconate.[3]

First, note that the council did not "restore" the diaconate at all, at least in the sense that we normally use the word *restore.* There have *always* been deacons in the church. What changed was the *way* in which the ministry of the deacon was exercised. For the first four or five centuries of the

2. *Sacrosanctum Concilium* (The Constitution on the Sacred Liturgy), 10. Translation by author.

3. See William T. Ditewig, "Charting a Theology of Diaconate: An Exercise in Ecclesial Cartography," in Owen F. Cummings, William T. Ditewig, Richard R. Gaillardetz, *Theology of the Diaconate: The State of the Question* (Mahwah, NJ: Paulist Press, 2005), esp. 49–54.

church, all deacons were "permanent" deacons. Later, the diaconate became simply a transitional stage a man passed through on his way to ordination as a priest. Theologically, of course, he *remained* a deacon, but in the lives of most priests this reality had little practical meaning. Thus, there was no need for a distinct theology of the diaconate apart from a theology of the presbyterate, since the presbyterate was the "end" of the diaconate. What Vatican II actually did was to restore the *permanence* of the diaconate, so that it was no longer a ministry that culminated in priesthood. The vital question then becomes, "Why did the bishops at Vatican II feel that a *permanent* diaconate was necessary in the contemporary church?" The bishops observed that the functions of deacons are "supremely necessary" for the life of the church, and that was the reason they were restoring its permanence. In short, then, Vatican II *renewed* the diaconate by *restoring* the permanence of its exercise.

The background to this historic decision is fascinating, but far too extensive to present here.[4] Nonetheless, there are several themes from the historical record that must be noted

---

4. See, for example, William T. Ditewig, "The Deacon as a Voice of Lament and Link to Thanksgiving and Justice," in *Liturgical Ministry* 13:1 (Winter 2004) 23–31, esp. 24–26; William T. Ditewig, *101 Questions and Answers on Deacons* [hereafter *Deacons*] (Mahwah, NJ: Paulist Press, 2004), 19–22; Josef Hornef, "The Genesis and Growth of the Proposal," in *Foundations for the Renewal of the Diaconate* (Washington, DC: United States Catholic Conference, 1993), 6; Margret Morche, *Zur Erneuerung des Ständigen Diakonats* (Freiburg: Lambertus-Verlag, 1996), esp. 15–21; Otto Pies, "Block 26: Erfahrungen aus dem Priesterleben in Dachau," *Stimmen der Zeit* 141 (1947–48): 10–28; and

for a proper understanding of the contemporary diaconate. First is the gradual recovery of the notion that the church herself is a servant-church in the world. This growing realization was documented in the nineteenth century in Germany, and became even more pronounced during the Second World War. In conversations prior to the war, during the war itself (especially at the Dachau Concentration Camp), and following the war, writers began to examine how the church might become a more effective witness to the world and prevent further violence, atrocities, and horror. The renewal of a permanent diaconal order was one of the suggestions discussed. Deacons were not needed primarily because of any shortage of priests (according to these writers), or because of any unique set of functions deacons might perform, but because the church needed a permanent sacramental sign of her own diaconal nature.

The bishops at Vatican II picked up this theme readily, and when speaking of deacons, described their ministry as a service of Word, sacrament, and charity. By his ordination, the deacon is to integrate, permanently and publicly, *diakonia, leitourgia,* and *martyria.* In short, through his own ministry and life, the deacon is to help the church see how these constitutive elements of church fit together.[5]

Perhaps nowhere is this more strongly stated than in the teaching of Popes Paul VI and John Paul II. In his homily to

---

Wilhelm Schamoni, *Familienväter als geweihte Diakone* (Paderborn: Schöningh, 1953); English translation: *Married Men as Ordained Deacons,* trans. Otto Eisner (London: Burns and Oates, 1955).

5. Ditewig, *Deacons,* 89–90.

the bishops of the Second Vatican Council on December 7, 1965, the day before the solemn closing of the council, Paul VI stated:

> We stress that the teaching of the council is chan-
> neled in one direction, the service of humankind, of
> every condition, in every weakness and need. The
> church has declared herself a servant of humanity at
> the very time when her teaching role and her pas-
> toral government have, by reason of this church
> solemnity, assumed greater splendor and vigor.
> However, the idea of service has been central.[6]

This realization finds a concrete sacramental expression within the renewed diaconate; Pope Paul VI would later write that the diaconate is a "driving force for the Church's *diakonia* and a sacrament of the Lord Christ himself, who 'came not to be served but to serve.'"[7] John Paul II, in a 1987 address to the U.S. diaconate community gathered in Detroit, made the following observation: "The service of the deacon is the church's service sacramentalized. Yours is not just one ministry among others, but it is truly meant to be, as Paul VI described it, a 'driving force' for the church's *diakonia*. You are meant to be living signs of the servanthood of Christ's church."[8]

---

6. Paul VI, *Hodie concilium, AAS* 58 (1966), 57–64.

7. Paul VI, Apostolic Letter *Ad Pascendum* (15 August 1972), citing Matt 20:28.

8. John Paul II, "Allocution to the Permanent Deacons and Their Wives Given at Detroit, MI (19 September 1987)," *Origins* 17 (1987): 327–29.

It is within this context of a diaconal church that the ministerial diaconate finds its own identity.

The Dangers of Functionalism

There is an unfortunate tendency in some quarters to view the deacon and his ministries almost exclusively by the functions he exercises. However, as we know only too well from experience in other areas of life, human beings are more than a sum of the functions they perform: there is more to being a spouse or parent than simply a listing of the day's activities; there is more to being a bishop, priest, or deacon than a simple list of the "faculties" one receives to do certain things. This tendency to focus on functions has sometimes led to two extremes with regard to the liturgical ministry of the deacon: either the liturgical ministry has been minimized as something not really critical to the deacon's supposed "real" functions of social service; or, conversely, parish-based sacramental ministry has become the principal activity of deacons, with almost no involvement in other areas of ministry.

A functional approach to the liturgy is particularly problematic, and opens the door to a variety of aberrations. For example, one might say that there is no *need* for the deacon to proclaim the Gospel; that others, including the priest, are fully capable of performing this function. Conclusion? There's no *need* for the deacon, since the *function* can be carried out legitimately by someone else. However, one might extend this argument to include lectors, suggesting that there's no real need for lectors since others (such as the priest, for example) could just as easily proclaim the readings. Since there is no unique function, therefore, the argument might conclude that there is no longer a need for lay persons to read the scriptures at Mass. I think most people would recognize the flaw here: ministry, including liturgical ministry, is a communion of a wide variety of persons and functions. The diversity of ministers underscores that very communion.

To understand the ministry of the deacon properly, one must overcome the extremes of functionalism and find a true theological balance between the three dimensions of the deacon's ministry: Word, sacrament, and servant-leadership.[9]

The Deacon's and the Bishop's Ministries

The Second Vatican Council describes the bishop's ministry as one of service *(diakonia)*. This ministry, which comes

---

9. A word about these terms is necessary. The Latin text refers to the threefold apostolic ministry as *munus docendi, munus sanctificandi,* and *munus regendi:* a ministry of teaching, sanctifying, and governing. This is sometimes simplified to "word, sacrament, and charity," which does not capture the full scope of the Latin, especially for the last category. I find it interesting that *regendi* is linked with *charity;* to me, this suggests a useful link between the notion of ecclesial leadership-in-service. One participates in ecclesial governance as an expression of *diakonia. Servant-leadership* is a term often associated with the ministry of the bishop. The tradition of the church has also consistently associated the ministries of the bishop and the deacon; indeed the deacon was ordainted, "not to priesthood, but for service to the bishop." Through his ordination, the deacon participates in the servant-leadership of the bishop. For this reason, *munus regendi* will be most often rendered as "servant-leadership" in this text.

to us from the apostles, is known as *apostolic ministry,* and it consists of a triple set of responsibilities: for Word (evangelization, preaching, and teaching), sacrament (presiding at the prayer of the people of God), and servant-leadership. Because of his ordination as bishop, the bishop has the fullness of these responsibilities, and he ordains two other groups of ministers to help him carry them out. Priests and deacons are ordained into a participation in the bishop's ministry, and *all* priests and *all* deacons have responsibilities for *all* three areas of ministry. Each order exercises these ministries in distinct ways, but all of the ordained have an obligation to exercise all of them in ways appropriate to their order. The bishops of the United States have been teaching of the intrinsic unity of the deacon's functions for more than twenty years. In fact, the *National Directory for the Formation, Ministry, and Life of Permanent Deacons in the United States,* promulgated in December 2004, cites its 1984 predecessor document directly when it proclaims: "The diaconal ministries [of Word, sacrament, and charity], distinguished above, are not to be separated; the deacon is ordained for them all, and no one should be ordained who is not prepared to undertake each in some way."[10] Finally, mention must be made of a most challenging paragraph from a recent document from the Holy See on the ministry of deacons:

---

10. United States Conference of Catholic Bishops, *The National Directory for the Formation, Ministry, and Life of Permanent Deacons in the United States* [hereafter *National Directory*](Washington, DC: USCCB, 2004), #39, citing the National Conference of Catholic Bishops, *Permanent Deacons in the United States: Guidelines on Their Formation and Ministry* (Washington, DC: USCC, 1985), #43.

In every case it is important, however, that deacons fully exercise their ministry, in preaching, in the liturgy and in charity to the extent that circumstances permit. They should not be relegated to marginal duties, be made merely to act as substitutes, nor discharge duties normally entrusted to non-ordained members of the faithful. Only in this way will the true identity of permanent deacons as ministers of Christ become apparent and the impression avoided that deacons are simply lay people particularly involved in the life of the Church.[11]

These citations, of course, apply to the full range of diaconal ministries, and are not limited to the liturgy alone. The instruction *Redemptionis Sacramentum* (On Certain Matters to Be Observed or to Be Avoided Regarding the Most Holy Eucharist) says, "Priests have also made solemn promises to exercise with fidelity their ministry, as have Deacons. They are expected to live up to their sacred responsibilities."[12] The same document later challenges, "Let all Deacons, then, do their part so that the Sacred Liturgy will be celebrated according to the norms of the duly approved liturgical books."[13] In the

---

11. Congregation for the Clergy, *Directory for the Ministry and Life of Permanent Deacons* [hereafter *Vatican Directory*] (Washington, DC: USCC, 1998), #40.

12. Congregation for Divine Worship and the Discipline of the Sacraments, Instruction on the Eucharist *Redemptionis Sacramentum: On Certain Matters to Be Observed or to Be Avoided Regarding the Most Holy Eucharist* (Washington, DC: United States Conference of Catholic Bishops, 2004), #4.

13. Ibid., #35.

practical experience of many deacons, however, the challenge to "fully exercise one's ministry" in the liturgy can be quite profound, and the challenge comes from both within the diaconal order and outside it. One deacon once told me quite sincerely, "I don't like to preach, and I think that deacons who like to preach aren't good deacons." And, yet, as outlined above and in liturgical documents, preaching at Mass and at other times is one of the functions expected of a deacon. In other cases, even when the deacon is fully capable and eager to exercise his ministry, other ministers decide that he will not. A classic example is when the presider tells the deacon before Mass that he (the presider) will proclaim the Gospel that day since the presider is giving the homily. Other examples abound, but this is not intended to be a list of diaconal complaints! Rather, it is a reminder to all involved with the liturgy that the proper roles and responsibilities of all the church's ministers, ordained and lay, ought to be respected and exercised to the fullest extent possible.

In the case of deacons, the participation in the apostolic ministry of the bishop has a uniquely diaconal character:

> Apostolic ministry, fully expressed sacramentally in the episcopal order, is to be characterized by an emptying of self for others. This is a ministry, like Christ's, of total self-sacrifice on behalf of others. Those who have a share in the apostolic ministry freely accept this aspect of Christ's identity as part of their own. Apostolic ministry is centered on the Eucharist: it flows from the minister's

participation in Christ's own sacrifice of himself, celebrated within the form of a sacred memorial meal. The *diakonia* of apostolic ministry is Eucharistic, a breaking and sharing of one's life for the building up of the body in memory of Christ. The ordination of the deacon into a share of the apostolic ministry is a reminder to all of the concrete ways in which the Christ Himself poured himself out for all. Such is the radical nature of the diaconate.[14]

Perhaps no contemporary theologian has expressed the intrinsic unity of the deacon's ministry more succinctly and eloquently than Cardinal Walter Kasper, theologian, former bishop of Rottenburg-Stuttgart, and Prefect of the Council for the Promotion of Christian Unity: "In his ministry of the altar, he [the deacon] lays the needs of human beings on the eucharistic table, and naturally he also speaks of these needs when he preaches. He must make the parish aware of urgent situations of need, motivating them to share with one another and to give practical help."[15]

---

14. William T. Ditewig, "The Deacon as a Voice of Lament and Link to Thanksgiving and Justice," in *Liturgical Ministry* 13 (Winter 2004), 29.

15. Walter Kasper, "The Diaconate," in *Leadership in the Church: How Traditional Roles Can Serve the Christian Community Today* (New York: Crossroad, 2003), 40.

The Eucharist as "Source and Summit" of the Deacon's Ministry and Life

It is clear that the deacon's liturgical ministry, like that of a priest, is one of three constitutive dimensions of his ministry. This can help overcome the dangers of functionalism: the Eucharist lies at the core of the deacon's identity and ministry, as with all disciples, but at the same time it does not exhaust the limits of his ministerial responsibilities. For all of Christ's faithful, obviously including deacons with their own unique responsibilities within the liturgy, the Eucharist is "the summit toward which the activity of the church is directed, and at the same time it is the font from which all her strength flows."[16] For this reason, the importance of the deacon's liturgical must never be minimized. Consider this citation from the 1998 *Vatican Directory:*

> The rite of ordination emphasizes another aspect of the diaconal ministry—ministry at the altar. Deacons receive the Sacrament of Orders, so as to serve as a vested minister in the sanctification of the Christian community, in hierarchical communion with the bishop and priests. They provide a sacramental assistance to the ministry of the bishop and, subordinately, to that of the priests which is intrinsic, fundamental and distinct. Clearly, this diaconia at the altar, since founded on the Sacrament of

---

16. *Sacrosanctum Concilium* (The Constitution on the Sacred Liturgy), #10. Translation by author.

Orders, differs in essence from any liturgical ministry entrusted to the lay faithful. The liturgical ministry of the deacon is also distinct from that of the ordained priestly ministry....Liturgical actions cannot be reduced to mere private or social actions which can be celebrated by anybody since they belong to the Body of the universal Church.[17]

The bishops of the United States echo and extend this sentiment:

For the Church gathered at worship, moreover, the ministry of the deacon is a visible, grace-filled sign of the integral connection between sharing at the Lord's Eucharistic table and serving the many hungers felt so keenly by all God's children. In the deacon's liturgical ministry, as in a mirror, the Church sees a reflection of her own diaconal character and is reminded of her mission to serve as Jesus did. In the context of the Church's public worship, because of its centrality in the life of the believing community, the ministry of the deacon in the threefold diakonia of the word, of the liturgy, and of charity is uniquely concentrated and integrated.[18]

The implications of these teachings are quite profound. Perhaps most fundamentally, they suggest that whenever possible, a deacon ought to be present and functioning at *every* Mass. Furthermore, the GIRM, in discussing the very nature of

---

17. *Vatican Directory,* ##28–29.
18. *National Directory,* ##33–34.

the Eucharist itself, refers to the Mass as "the action of Christ and the People of God arrayed hierarchically" (16). Gerard Moore observes, "All the members of the Church are allocated a place in this order, which secures their rights and sets out their obligations."[19] One's place in this order flows from sacramental initiation and, for the ordained, from their ordination as well. As an ordained member of this hierarchical communion, the deacon has his proper place at the Eucharistic Table, and the deacon's exercise of his liturgical ministry at Mass is at the heart of the Eucharist and at the heart of his own individual and ecclesial identity. Therefore, every Mass should have a deacon, whenever possible. This would be quite easy to achieve in areas which are blessed with more than one deacon in a parish. Just as we often expect our priests to exercise their Eucharistic ministry at more than one Mass on a weekend, such an expectation is reasonable for our deacons as well. Deacons, who serve in the person of Christ and in the name of the Church through their ordination and their participation in the apostolic ministry of the bishop, have a public and permanent responsibility for serving the People of God assembled for the very act that constitutes their sacred identity as Church.

Conversely, it must also be recognized that exercising a liturgical ministry without allowing the Eucharist to find extended expression in ministries of Word and servant-leadership will also distort the sacramental identity and mission of

---

19. Gerard Moore, *Understanding the General Instruction of the Roman Missal* (Mahwah, NJ: Paulist Press, 2007).

the deacon. There is an inherent unity between the three dimensions of apostolic ministry, and the deacon must attend to all three, with the Eucharist at the core of his being. Not only must deacons themselves never lose sight of this fact; others involved in the liturgy and its planning must recognize it as well.

The Deacon and the New GIRM

As discussed above, the diaconate *never* disappeared; rather, it was transformed and redefined into a transitory stage on the way to ultimate ordination into the presbyterate. The diaconate ceased being described on its own terms and began being defined and described by its relationship to the presbyterate, its ultimate end. The paradigm for discussions of ordained ministry, therefore, has been primarily sacerdotal, and in particular presbyteral, ministry. Other ministries, including the episcopate and diaconate (as well as various forms of lay ecclesial ministry), are often still measured against this paradigm.[20] Using such a frame of reference, ministries other than the presbyterate are often described in terms of what they are *not:* the laity are described as "*non*ordained"; and while deacons are ordained, they do *not* "say

____

20. This may be seen in recent statements from the Holy See, such as the multidicasterial "Instruction on Certain Questions Regarding the Collaboration of the Non-Ordained Faithful in the Sacred Ministry of the Priest" (Vatican City: Libreria Editrice Vaticana, 1997). Notice that even in the title, the laity are not referred to according to their baptismal status but rather according to what they are not. This practice is not unique to this document.

Mass," do *not* "hear confessions," and do *not* "give last rites." This method of negative identification must be overcome if the diaconate is to develop into the "proper and permanent" order desired and described by the council.

The late canonist James H. Provost once observed, when writing about the diaconate in the 1983 Code of Canon Law, "there is still no coherent treatment of permanent deacons as a 'proper and permanent rank of the hierarchy' comparable to the treatment given presbyters and bishops in the code; rather, they are treated as exceptions to the norms for presbyters."[21] One might extend this observation and concern to the liturgical ministries of the deacon as the church regains experience with this renewed order.

Consider the simple fact that the *Missale Romanum* has gone through three editions since the Second Vatican Council: the first in 1970, the second in 1975, and the latest in 2000 (it is for this latest edition of the Missal that the current GIRM has been promulgated). The first ordinations of permanent deacons took place in Germany in 1969; by the time of the first edition of the 1970 *Roman Missal* there were fewer than one hundred permanent deacons serving around the world; in the United States, there were only two! There are now more than 32,000 deacons serving worldwide, with more than 15,000 in the United States alone.[22] At the beginning of con-

---

21. James H. Provost, "Permanent Deacons in the 1983 Code," in *Canon Law Society of America Proceedings* 46 (1984), 175.

22. These data are reflected in the files of the Secretariat for the Diaconate at the United States Conference of Catholic Bishops and of the International Diaconate Center in Rottenburg, Germany.

temporary revisions to the *Missal,* the only deacons around were still the so-called transitional deacons just as before the council; however, now the church has had more than thirty-five years of experience with this renewed order of ministry. On the one hand, one may be pleased by the increasing appreciation of the liturgical dimensions of the diaconal ministry within the *Missal,* such as the development of an entire section of the GIRM on the celebration of Mass based on the presence and ministry of the deacon. On the other hand, however, one notes a certain ambivalence in the text itself since this section is placed *after* a section on the celebration of Mass *without* a deacon! Therefore, while we seem to be moving away from an understanding of the role of the deacon at Mass as a liturgical expression of the medieval *cursus honorum* (until 1972, the pattern of rising "through the ranks" from the minor orders of porter, lector, exorcist, and acolyte, and the major orders of subdeacon and deacon, culminating with ordination as priest), we have not yet arrived at a fully mature understanding of the deacon-at-Mass as sign of the church's own *diakonia.* On this point, writing about the diaconate, Gerard Moore has written,

> As well, whereas the *Instruction* contains a developed theology of the *sacerdos,* there is little about the deacon. There is simply the acknowledgement that the order has been held in high honor since apostolic times, and that the deacon has his own proper functions. Ultimately our liturgical theology and practice about the function of those in sacred orders at Mass is focused on the priest, the

sacerdos. Consequently, our thinking is truncated, and the manifestation of the church arrayed hierarchically restricted.[23]

Therefore, we may conclude, echoing Provost, that while much progress has been made in the integration of the deacon into the contemporary *Missal,* additional work remains to be done in future editions.

Conclusions

This then is how the liturgical role of the deacon might be understood. When the deacon enters the assembly holding aloft the Book of the Gospels, he serves to bring Christ the Good News to the community without uttering a word. If he articulates parts of the penitential rite, he speaks the concerns of all and the constant hope for God's mercy. As the primary liturgical herald of the Gospel, commissioned as such during his ordination, the deacon can demonstrate the unbreakable link between the Gospel of the Lord and the diaconal responsibility of the entire Church to respond in justice. When the deacon offers the General Intercessions, he should be naming the very concrete and messy daily needs of the people. When the deacon preaches, his preaching should be of a different kind than that of other ministers; the deacon's homilies should be particularly prophetic, calling the people to be true to the diaconal responsibility of initiation,

---

23. Moore, *Understanding the General Instruction*, 91.

to take the Gospel out of the assembly and into the world at large. During the preparation of the wine, it is the deacon's responsibility to add water to the wine with the words, "By the mystery of this water and wine may we come to share in the divinity of Christ, who humbled himself to share in our humanity." This simple act and these simple words capture the communion of Christ and church, Christ's kenotic and salvific assumption of human nature, and the transformative power of the Eucharist. Given the nature of the diaconate as discussed above, I believe that this simple ritual action is one of the most significant assigned to the deacon during the Eucharist. And as the deacon exhorts the people to prayer, or directs various elements of the liturgy, he models servant-leadership and demonstrates anew Christ's injunction that the love and worship of God is linked perpetually to the promotion of justice, care, and peace for those most in need. Simply phrased: we can't truly love God if we don't also love our neighbor.

At the dismissal, it is the deacon who sends the assembly forth, back into the world in need of Christ's kenotic, transformative, and salvific love. Truly, the deacon ought to model in his person, his life, and his ministry the words of the Letter of James: "Religion that is pure and undefiled before God, the Father, is this: to care for orphans and widows in their distress, and to keep oneself unstained by the world" (Jas 1:27).

CHAPTER ONE

Preparation and Planning

—————

Principles and Commentary

The Role of the Deacon at Mass

The *General Instruction of the Roman Missal* (GIRM) summarizes the nature of the deacon's liturgical ministry: "After the priest, the deacon, in virtue of the sacred ordination he has received, holds first place among those who minister in the Eucharistic Celebration. For the sacred Order of the diaconate has been held in high honor in the Church even from the time of the Apostles" (94). The GIRM presumes that when a deacon is present at Mass, he will function liturgically at that Mass. This is quite clear in GIRM 171, where the deacon's role is again summarized:

> 171. When he is present at the Eucharistic Celebration, a deacon should exercise his ministry, wearing sacred vestments. For the deacon
>
> a. Assists the priest and remains at his side;
> b. Ministers at the altar, with the chalice as well as the book;

    c. Proclaims the Gospel and, at the direction of the priest celebrant, may preach the homily;

    d. Guides the faithful by appropriate introductions and explanations, and announces the intentions of the Prayer of the Faithful;

    e. Assists the priest celebrant in distributing Communion, and purifies and arranges the sacred vessels;

    f. As needed, fulfills the duties of other ministers himself if none of them is present.

However, this presumption that the deacon functions liturgically at Mass must be addressed in greater detail. It is an unfortunate practice in some places that this does not happen. Sometimes this is due to inadequate formation in which the liturgical role of the deacon has been somewhat minimized, even to the extent of suggesting that a deacon's liturgical and catechetical roles are of lesser significance than his ministry of charity. In other situations, even when the deacon desires to assist liturgically, he is discouraged from doing so by his pastor or others, for a variety of reasons. As discussed in the introduction to this book, all persons involved in the liturgy need to appreciate the fact that the deacon's liturgical ministry is one of three constitutive elements of the deacon's ministry and life, just as it is for the priest and the bishop. The deacon's ordination, among other things, conveys to him a permanent responsibility and obligation for his share of the church's worship just as binding as the other commitments assumed at ordination.

Some phrase the question as, "Does this mean that the deacon exercises his liturgical ministry at *every* Mass?" I prefer to approach the matter from a different perspective. It seems more helpful to operate from the premise that every Mass ought to have the liturgical presence of *all* of the church's ministers, including the deacon. For example, even at a daily Mass we generally have lay persons serving in their variety of roles in addition to the priest serving in his role; this is considered normative. It is, or ought to be, just as normative for the deacon to be present and to assist. In parishes with the services of more than one deacon, scheduling a deacon for most Masses poses less of a problem than a parish with only one deacon. Nonetheless, the ideal ought to be that a deacon assist at each Mass, making our question really, "Given what we believe and teach about the very nature of the Eucharist and its centrality in our Catholic identity, why *wouldn't* there be a deacon at every Mass?"

Especially for a married deacon, this expectation can be a source of tension in his family, who prior to his ordination has been accustomed to attending Mass with him. This has sometimes contributed to the practice of a deacon assisting liturgically at Mass only on rare or special occasions. While the deacon's attending Mass with his family is certainly laudable, it can also contribute to catechetical confusion if the deacon only rarely exercises his liturgical functions. While the deacon has a responsibility to and for his family, he has taken on additional responsibilities for the entire community as well, and these must not be ignored either. The result is that the deacon may need to attend more than one Mass a weekend, perhaps attending one Mass with his family and assisting at others. It is also important to recall that attending Mass together need not mean that the members of the family are in the same pew! Many families take on various liturgical roles within the Mass: some of the children may be altar servers, for example, while their mother is in the choir and their father serves as deacon.

When I was growing up in the Midwest in the 1950s, I recall an occasion when Sister announced to our class that the following Sunday a Maronite priest would be celebrating the Divine Liturgy in our parish. As she described the differences between the Latin Mass and the Maronite Liturgy, some of us who were altar servers begged to be allowed to serve. Sister's response came as quite a shock to our sixth-grade ears and experience, as she explained that "Father's sons will be serving." For most if not all of us, this was the first time we realized that many Eastern Catholic priests were married with families! Their responsibilities as priest, husband, and father blend rather naturally, and the same can be true of the married deacon and his family.

As a married deacon myself, I realize how difficult this balancing act can be. Early in my ministry as a deacon, I decided to attend Mass with my family. Shortly after Mass, I was approached by a number of people who shared with me how sad they were that I had quit the diaconate! They told me that they would be praying for us so that I would return to ministry. Now while this was a good catechetical moment to explain the various responsibilities of the deacon's life, it was also helpful to me in realizing just how essential the deacon's public responsibilities are. While the married deacon's family responsibilities are critically important, so too are the responsibilities taken on at ordination; neither set of responsibilities can be treated lightly.

Another citation from the GIRM provides the scope of the deacon's liturgical ministry at Mass: "All, therefore, whether they are ordained ministers or lay Christian faithful, in fulfilling their office or their duty, should carry out solely but completely that which pertains to them."[1] The phrase "solely but completely" is extremely important for the entire worshipping community, including of course the deacon. While there is often a good understanding of what constitutes a particular minister's *sole* responsibility for some aspect of the Mass, sometimes the notion of *completeness* eludes us in practice. For example, most people recognize that it is the deacon's responsibility to proclaim the Gospel at Mass; what other liturgical responsibilities are rightly exercised by the deacon might be more mysterious. Throughout this book, every effort will be made to address this issue, so that the full range of diaconal function may be appreciated.

To summarize the deacon's role: his responsibilities at Mass flow from sacramental ordination. This is not to be understood in terms of privilege or status, but of service. All ministry, and in a special way the ministry of the ordained, is

---

1. GIRM 91, citing *Sacrosanctum Concilium* 26.

by definition a form of service. Ordination is a permanent and public call to serve the entire church in the person of Christ and in the name of the church, and this service is expressed and constituted through the Eucharistic Celebration itself. Put another way, the participation of the deacon in liturgy is not an optional, personal ministry that the deacon may choose to exercise or not. Just as with the bishop and his priests, the deacon has the liturgy at the core of his identity and responsibility.[2] It is critically important that this point be appreciated by all priests, especially pastors, deacons, and everyone involved in the planning of liturgies. The GIRM outlines this ministry in general terms as follows:

> At Mass the deacon has his own part in proclaiming the Gospel, in preaching God's word from time to time, in announcing the intentions of the Prayer of the Faithful, in ministering to the priest, in preparing the altar and serving the celebration of the Sacrifice, in distributing the Eucharist to the faithful, especially under the species of wine, and sometimes in giving directions regarding the people's gestures and posture. (94)

---

2. It is significant to note that in the GIRM's section on concelebration, #208 directs that if a deacon is not present at a concelebrated Mass, "his proper duties are to be carried out by some of the concelebrants." This is in contrast with the next sentence, which addresses the absence of "other ministers" (lay ministers, such as lectors, cantors, and so on), in which the GIRM directs that the proper parts of these other ministers "may be entrusted to other suitable members of the faithful; otherwise, they are carried out by some of the concelebrants." In short, if a deacon is absent, only other ordained ministers may exercise his functions.

If there are several persons present who are able to exercise the same ministry, nothing forbids their distributing among themselves and performing different parts of the same ministry or duty. For example, one deacon may be assigned to take the sung parts, another to serve at the altar; if there are several readings, it is well to distribute them among a number of lectors. The same applies for the other ministries. (109)

The Deacon and the Elements of the Mass

What follows is an overview of various elements of the Mass presented in the GIRM. Some of these paragraphs relate directly and specifically to the deacon; others apply indirectly. *All* of them are important sources of information and reflection, and will be examined in greater detail in subsequent chapters.

> *Reading and Explaining the Word of God (29)*
> 29. When the Sacred Scriptures are read in the Church, God himself speaks to his people, and Christ, present in his own word, proclaims the Gospel....[A] fuller understanding and a greater effectiveness of the word is fostered by a living commentary on the word, that is, the homily, as part of the liturgical action.

Throughout the Mass, it is Christ who acts: in and through the assembly, in and through the proclaimed Word, in and through the ordained ministers, and in and through the Eucharistic elements themselves.[3] Paragraph 29 makes this abundantly clear in its presentation on the scripture readings and the homily. The deacon is the ordinary minister of the Gospel, as will be examined later: even when the diocesan bishop—or the Pope!—celebrates the Mass, it is still the deacon's responsibility to proclaim the Gospel. (While on active duty as a Navy commander, I once visited a Navy chapel in which no deacon had ever before served. Before Mass began, the chaplain decided to explain a few things to the assembly. Regarding the Gospel, he remarked, "You'll notice today that Deacon Bill will proclaim the Gospel, not me. That's because when a deacon is present at Mass, he outranks the priest on that score!" Now while one might object to his use of military "rank" language, in this instance it was quite helpful to the assembly in question!) The above passage from the GIRM also makes quite clear that it is not the deacon who proclaims his own good news to the assembly, but Christ—using the deacon as his instrument—who proclaims the Good News of salvation. Likewise, the deacon shares in the responsibility to offer a "living commentary" on the Word proclaimed through the homily.

The Prayers and Other Parts Pertaining to the Priest

At first the three paragraphs of the GIRM under this heading (31–33) may seem inapplicable to the deacon. However, two points must be made. First, these paragraphs

---

3. See *Sacrosanctum Concilium* 10.

can help the deacon distinguish the presidential responsibilities of the bishop or priest from his own diaconal responsibilities. Second, there are important insights in these paragraphs that *do* apply in varying degrees to the deacon. For example, GIRM 31 reminds presiders that, "where it is indicated in the rubrics, the celebrant is permitted to adapt them somewhat in order that they respond to the understanding of those participating. However, he should always take care to keep to the sense of the text given in the *Missal* and to express it succinctly." There are times when the deacon addresses the assembly (e.g., the Greeting of, or Sign of, Peace, the Dismissal) in which these words have similar relevance. While the rubrics might indicate some measure of adaptation, the deacon, like the priest, is well-advised to "keep to the sense of the text" and "to express it succinctly."

The Vocal Expression of the Different Texts
38. In texts that are to be spoken in a loud and clear voice, whether by the priest or the deacon, or by the lector, or by all, the tone of voice should correspond to the genre of the text itself, that is, depending upon whether it is a reading, a prayer, a commentary, an acclamation, or a sung text; the tone should also be suited to the form of celebration and to the solemnity of the gathering. Consideration should also be given to the idiom of different languages and the culture of different peoples.

In the rubrics and in the norms that follow, words such as "say" and "proclaim" are to be understood

of both singing and reciting, according to the principles just stated above.

The applicability of this paragraph to the deacon is
straightforward. The *Vatican Directory* observes that diaconal
ordination is the "font of sacramental grace" that nourishes
the deacon's entire ministry, and that "careful and profound
theological and liturgical preparation must precede reception
of that grade to enable the deacon to participate worthily in
the celebration of the sacraments and sacramentals."[4]
Formation programs preparing candidates for ordination to
the diaconate should ensure that candidates are capable of
adapting themselves according to the demands of the liturgy
and the nature of the particular assembly. In particular, candidates must be well-versed and competent in communicating
the various elements, rhythm, and pace of the liturgy.[5]

The Importance of Singing
[The great importance of singing within the liturgy
is covered in GIRM 39–41, with 40 specifying that
in] the choosing of the parts actually to be sung,
however, preference should be given to those that
are of greater importance *and especially to those
to be sung by the priest or the deacon or the lector.* (emphasis added)

---

4. *Vatican Directory,* #28.
5. In a "Secondary Document" promulgated concurrent with the
2004 *National Directory,* the bishops of the United States offer model
standards of readiness, which include a number of competencies related to
the liturgical formation of candidates for ordination.

In the medieval church, one's ability to sing well was sometimes seen as a sign of a vocation to the diaconate, which had become largely a liturgical and ceremonial office. While the ability to sing well is no longer given that kind of weight—for which we are all most grateful!—that does not relieve the deacon of the responsibility to sing on occasion. Nothing could be worse or more anticlimactic, for example, on Easter Sunday morning than for the deacon, after a Mass full of joyous *Alleluias*, to dismiss the assembly with a *spoken* dismissal. Some deacons believe that because they do not possess any musical ability, this simple fact somehow absolves them of any responsibility to try. The church is graced by many ordained ministers who will never sing with the Metropolitan Opera; still, our liturgy *demands* that, on occasion, certain parts are to be sung, and this includes parts assigned to the deacon. Just as we expect other ordained ministers to sing, even minimally, so too the deacon is expected to sing. These paragraphs serve as a reminder to all that the purpose and goal of singing in the liturgy is for all present to proclaim the glory of God using the language of song.

Movements and Posture

42. The gestures and posture of the priest, the deacon, and the ministers, as well as those of the people, ought to contribute to making the entire celebration resplendent with beauty and noble simplicity, so that the true and full meaning of the different parts of the celebration is evident and that

the participation of all is fostered. Therefore, attention should be paid to what is determined by this General Instruction and the traditional practice of the Roman Rite and to what serves the common spiritual good of the People of God, rather than private inclination or arbitrary choice. (42)

This whole section of the GIRM (42–44) reflects both the art and the science of liturgy. Notice the desire that the celebration is to be "resplendent with beauty and noble simplicity," to enhance the "full, conscious and active participation" of the entire assembly. At the same time, individual liturgical ministers are not to follow their own personal insights or preferences; rather, they are to plumb the riches of the rites themselves. Perhaps a musical analogy would be helpful.

Experienced musicians are called upon to express through their own skill and musicianship the meaning and inspiration of the composer. Still, while there is considerable freedom given to the musician to interpret the music, that freedom is not absolute. The musician cannot change the notes or the structures of the composition. Similarly, liturgical ministers are given a range of expression within the "text" of the liturgy itself, and just as the musician finds the heart of the composer's vision within the parameters of the music itself, so too does the liturgical minister find the heart of the Eucharistic Celebration within the liturgy itself.

Silence
Sacred silence also, as part of the celebration, is to be observed at the designated times. Its purpose,

however, depends on the time it occurs in each part of the celebration. Thus within the Act of Penitence and again after the invitation to pray, all recollect themselves; but at the conclusion of a reading or the homily, all meditate briefly on what they have heard; then after Communion, they praise and pray to God in their hearts.

Even before the celebration itself, it is commendable that silence [is] to be observed in the church, in the sacristy, in the vesting room, and in adjacent areas, so that all may dispose themselves to carry out the sacred action in a devout and fitting manner. (45)

As will be explored in more detail in subsequent chapters, the observation of silence is often a part of the deacon's liturgical ministry. This is particularly true during the Penitential Rite, after the readings and homily, and after communion. In some cases, this means that the deacon should simply not rush to the next line to be spoken (such as during the Penitential Rite); in other cases, it means being attentive and reflective, and not becoming distracted with related activities. One of the most powerful contributions of the deacon's ministry can be his own modeling of appropriate liturgical behavior. Silence is an important component of this.

At times the observation of a period of silence can be more difficult than might be expected. In my own experience, this is particularly true during the Penitential Rite since certain forms demand close cooperation and a good sense of timing between the presider, deacon, and assembly. If the presider has just invited the entire assembly to "call to mind our sins," the deacon ought to wait and give the assembly (and himself!) time to do just that. Still, some presiders get nervous and impatient (especially if he and the deacon have not discussed this in advance, and the presider is perhaps worried that the deacon has actually *forgotten* his next line), and the assembly begins to wonder what the delay is all about. It is the experience of a number of deacons, when they pause at this point of the Mass, to be teased after Mass by parishioners who think that he forgot his lines! The solution, of course, is to coordinate the details of such moments of silence in advance with the presider, and to provide occasional reminders to the rest of the assembly about the value of silence, and, just as important, when such periods of silence are going to occur during the Mass.

Vestments

Paragraph 119 of the GIRM describes the vestments to be prepared in the sacristy before Mass. For the deacon, this includes the amice, alb, cincture, stole, and dalmatic; the amice and cincture are *not* required if they are not needed due to the form of the alb. (Description of the deacon's vestments are in the Appendix.)

The dalmatic is an ancient vestment associated with a servant, and it is the unique vestment of the deacon as well as the bishop, who for certain celebrations (such as ordinations) may wear the dalmatic under the chasuble. Before the liturgical reforms following the Second Vatican Council, especially at Solemn High Masses, the priest wore the chasuble, the deacon the dalmatic, and the subdeacon the tunicle; deacons and subdeacons *never* assisted at Mass vested only in alb and stole.[6] As styles of vestments evolved after the council, and with the elimination of Solemn High Masses from the Roman Missal, along with the suppression of the subdiaconate in the Latin Church, very few vestment makers bothered to replace the deacon's vestments. This was especially true since at that time there were few permanent deacons assuming their responsibilities; in other words, in the late 1960s and early 1970s there was no perceived pressing need for deacon's vestments and, consequently, few were available.

It is my opinion that all of this contributed in some measure to the successive editions of the GIRM permitting the omission of the dalmatic "out of necessity or on account of a lesser degree of solemnity" (119). "Necessity" of course would refer, among other things, to the actual unavailability of the dalmatic. A "lesser degree of solemnity" is a bit harder to define, especially today when categories of Low Mass, High Mass, and Solemn High Mass no longer apply. Certainly the circumstances surrounding a particular celebration of the Eucharist may indicate an occasion of greater or lesser solemnity, but the Eucharist itself remains the same.

---

6. Except for seminarians who had actually been ordained to these orders, these "deacons" and "subdeacons" were usually priests who took on these liturgical roles for a particular Mass. It was not unusual, for example, to speak with a priest who would tell you that he was "deaconing" the Solemn High Mass on Sunday. This practice is, of course, no longer permitted.

The Eucharist celebrated during the Easter Vigil, with all of its various components and rituals, is still the same Mass that is celebrated every Sunday and indeed every weekday. So, what might be made of this remark of the GIRM about greater or lesser "degrees of solemnity"? This text is not the place to engage in any sort of substantive analysis of this question, but I believe there is a simple, straightforward, and practical response with regard to the question. The dalmatic is to the deacon what the chasuble is to the priest: it is the outer vestment normally worn for the Eucharist. Are there rare occasions when the priest may elect, due to "necessity or lesser degree of solemnity," to omit the chasuble? For example, the priest may decide that at a daily Mass cele-brated in a remote area he will forego the chasuble. Notice the extraordinary circumstances that would be present in such a case. It is my opinion that this same level of excep-tionality applies in a decision to omit the dalmatic. Simply put: *If the priest presiding at Mass is wearing the chasuble, the deacon(s) of the Mass wears the dalmatic.* I believe this is consistent with the language of the GIRM, and it also helps to explain the recent observation in *Redemptionis Sacramentum* 125 that "the proper vestment of the deacon is the dalmatic, to be worn over an alb and stole. In order that the beautiful tradition of the church may be preserved, it is praiseworthy to refrain from exercising the option of omitting the dalmatic."

It may seem curious that so much of my attention is being paid to the dalmatic. I am doing so for two reasons.

First, we are a church that makes rich use of outward signs and other aids to religious imagination and expression. Vestments do many things, including offering a link to our religious heritage. The alb, for example, is a sign and reminder of the white garment of baptism. The stole and dalmatic of the deacon express his servanthood as well as the servanthood of the entire church in the servanthood of Christ, just as the priest's vestments signal the priesthood of the priest and the church in the High Priesthood of Christ. The partnership of priest and deacon thus demonstrates to the assembly the link between priesthood and service; between worship of God and care of neighbor; between Word, sacrament, and charity.

The second reason for addressing this issue is far more practical. Increasing the use of the dalmatic can cause a practical financial problem for most deacons. In many parishes and dioceses, deacons provide (read: *pay for*) their own vestments on a routine basis. While priests and bishops may also own their own personal vestments, it is nonetheless the practice that the parish also provides standardized vestment sets. Dalmatics and matching stoles can be quite expensive, and increasingly dioceses are reminding their parishes that they have a responsibility to provide vestments for *all* of their ministers, including deacons. Certainly a deacon *may* purchase his own vestments or have them made, but the larger issue here is that the church has a responsibility to provide suitable vesture for her ministers. Just as the parish provides vestments for its priests, altar servers, and choir, it should also provide vestments for its deacons. *Redemptionis sacra-*

mentum directs, "Ordinaries should take care that in all churches and oratories subject to their jurisdiction there is present an adequate supply of liturgical vestments made in accordance with the norms."[7]

For additional background on the liturgical vestments used by deacons, please see the Appendix.

Conclusions

In the local Church, first place should certainly be given, because of its significance, to the Mass at which the Bishop presides, surrounded by his pres-byterate, deacons, and lay ministers, and in which the holy people of God participate fully and actively, for it is there that the preeminent expres-sion of the Church is found. (GIRM 112)

This paragraph echoes the teaching of the Second Vatican Council, which states that it is around the altar table of the bishop, surrounded by his ministers and the people, that the one, holy, catholic, and apostolic church is to be found (*LG* 26). In short, it is here that the entire *communio*, in all of its orders and diversity, finds the "preeminent expres-sion" of its sacramental identity. Deacons are an essential, vital component in this identity.

By ordination, deacons are consecrated by the Spirit and ordered to the service of the church as a participant in the

---

7. *Redemptionis sacramentum* 126.

apostolic ministry of the bishop, and all of his various liturgical ministries may be interpreted in light of this service. The deacon is a sacramental sign of Christ the Servant, witnessing to the entire church's identity as servant to the world.[8] While others also give such witness in various ways, it is the permanent and public responsibility of the deacon. As seen earlier, *Redemptionis Sacramentum* observes that, like priests, deacons "have also made solemn promises to exercise with fidelity their ministry," and that they too "are expected to live up to their sacred responsibilities."[9] Not only must deacons live up to their obligations in this regard, others involved in liturgical planning must understand these obligations and permit and encourage the deacon to exercise his full ministry.

For these reasons, therefore, the liturgical ministry of the deacon must never be seen as something optional or necessary only when "greater solemnity" is desired. For example, some priests and even some deacons (and others) have remarked that deacons need not assist at a daily Mass, because "there's no need; Father can handle it without help." But such an observation approaches liturgy simply as a set of

---

8. Referring to the deacon as an icon of Christ the Servant (Christ the Deacon) is becoming increasingly common in both official documents and in theological discourse. See, for example, Congregation for Catholic Education, *Basic Norms for the Formation of Permanent Deacons* (Vatican City: Libreria Editrice Vaticana, 1998), ##5, 11, 72; the *Vatican Directory* ##32, 38, 43, 45, 47, 49, 50, 57, 64, 67. See Owen F. Cummings, *Deacons and the Church* (Mahwah, NJ: Paulist Press, 2004), especially 20–29.

9. *Redemptionis Sacramentum,* Introduction 4.

functions to be determined by need rather than a tapestry of integrated ministries expressing the very *communio* of the church. *Diakonia* is a constitutive element of the church herself; that means we cannot be church without it. Since the Mass is the act by which the very church is constituted, it stands to reason that all constitutive elements be fully expressed sacramentally.

Questions for Reflection and Future Planning

1. The deacon's liturgical ministry flows from the broader nature of the diaconate itself. How well does your diocesan church and the parish understand the sacramental nature and the ministries of the diaconate? How might this catechesis be expanded and extended if necessary?

2. How is the nature and ministry of the deacon considered when planning parish and diocesan liturgies? Is it considered an optional dimension of liturgy, or is the complete ministry of the deacon seen as an essential element the liturgy?

3. Is the ministry of the deacon represented in liturgical planning structures for diocese and parish?

4. What vestments are the deacons in your parish wearing? Is the dalmatic worn by the deacon when assisting at a Mass in which the priest-presider is wearing a chasuble?

CHAPTER TWO

Introductory Rites

Principles and Commentary

For easy reference, this chapter will begin with selected citations from the GIRM concerning the deacon's role at Mass. This is followed by commentary.

Text of the GIRM on the Introductory Rites

46. The rites preceding the Liturgy of the Word, namely the Entrance, Greeting, Act of Penitence, *Kyrie, Gloria,* and Collect, have the character of a beginning, introduction, and preparation. Their purpose is to ensure that the faithful who come together as one establish communion and dispose themselves to listen properly to God's word and to celebrate the Eucharist worthily. In certain celebrations that are combined with Mass according to the norms of the liturgical books, the Introductory Rites are omitted or performed in a particular way.

The Entrance
47. After the people have gathered, the Entrance chant begins as the priest enters with the deacon and ministers....

172. Carrying the Book of the Gospels slightly elevated, the deacon precedes the priest as he approaches the altar or else walks at the priest's side.

Greeting of the Altar and of the People Gathered Together
49. When they reach the sanctuary, the priest, the deacon, and the ministers reverence the altar with a profound bow. As an expression of veneration, moreover, the priest and deacon then kiss the altar itself; as the occasion suggests, the priest also incenses the cross and the altar.

50. When the Entrance chant is concluded, the priest stands at the chair and, together with the whole gathering, makes the Sign of the Cross. Then he signifies the presence of the Lord to the community gathered there by means of the Greeting. By this Greeting and the people's response, the mystery of the Church gathered together is made manifest. After the greeting of the people, the priest, the deacon, or a lay minister may very briefly introduce the faithful to the Mass of the day.

173. When he [the deacon] reaches the altar, if he is carrying the Book of the Gospels, he omits the sign of reverence and goes up to the altar. It is particularly appropriate that he should place the Book of the Gospels on the altar, after which, together with the priest, he venerates the altar with a kiss. If, however, he is not carrying the Book of the Gospels, he makes a profound bow to

the altar with the priest in the customary way and with him venerates the altar with a kiss. Lastly, if incense is used, he assists the priest in putting some into the thurible and in incensing the cross and the altar.

174. After the incensation of the altar, he goes to the chair together with the priest, takes his place there at the side of the priest and assists him as necessary.

The Act of Penitence
51. Then the priest invites those present to take part in the Act of Penitence, which, after a brief pause for silence, the entire community carries out through a formula of general confession. The rite concludes with the priest's absolution, which, however, lacks the efficacy of the Sacrament of Penance.

The Kyrie Eleison
52. After the Act of Penitence, the *Kyrie* is always begun, unless it has already been included as part of the Act of Penitence. Since it is a chant by which the faithful acclaim the Lord and implore his mercy, it is ordinarily done by all, that is, by the people and with the choir or cantor having a part in it. As a rule, each acclamation is sung or said twice, though it may be repeated several times, by reason of the character of the various languages, as well as of the artistry of the music or of other circumstances. When the *Kyrie* is sung as a part of

the Act of Penitence, a trope may precede each acclamation.

The Gloria

53. The *Gloria* is a very ancient and venerable hymn in which the Church, gathered together in the Holy Spirit, glorifies and entreats God the Father and the Lamb. The text of this hymn may not be replaced by any other text. The *Gloria* is intoned by the priest or, if appropriate, by a cantor or by the choir; but it is sung either by everyone together, or by the people alternately with the choir, or by the choir alone. If not sung, it is to be recited either by all together or by two parts of the congregation responding one to the other. It is sung or said on Sundays outside the Seasons of Advent and Lent, on solemnities and feasts, and at special celebrations of a more solemn character.

The Collect

54. Next the priest invites the people to pray. All, together with the priest, observe a brief silence so that they may be conscious of the fact that they are in God's presence and may formulate their petitions mentally. Then the priest says the prayer which is customarily known as the Collect and through which the character of the celebration is expressed. In accordance with the ancient tradition of the Church, the collect prayer is usually addressed to God the Father, through Christ, in the Holy Spirit, and is concluded with a trinitarian, that is to say the longer, ending.

Commentary

The Introductory Rites of the Mass consist of the Entrance, Greeting, Act of Penitence, *Kyrie, Gloria,* and Collect (Opening Prayer). "Their purpose is to ensure that the faithful who come together as one establish communion and dispose themselves to listen properly to God's word and to celebrate the Eucharist worthily" (46). The following comments highlight the deacon's participation in these rites.

The first act of the Eucharistic Celebration is the gathering of the worshipping assembly. As the priest, deacon, and other ministers enter, the gathering of the assembly is complete, and the celebration begins in song. The Second Vatican Council teaches that

> in any community of the altar, under the sacred ministry of the bishop, there is exhibited a symbol of that charity and "unity of the Mystical Body, without which there can be no salvation." In these communities, though frequently small and poor, or widely scattered, Christ is present in whose power there is brought together one, holy, catholic, and apostolic church. For "the participation in the body and blood of Christ does nothing other than transform us into that which we consume."[1]

The theological significance of the act of gathering is not to be underestimated. As we saw in the last chapter in discussion

---

1. *Lumen gentium* (The Dogmatic Constitution on the Church) 26. Translation by author.

(GIRM 112), the celebration of the Eucharist is the "preeminent expression" of the church herself. The gathering of the *communio*, therefore, is a concrete expression of Vatican II's teaching: a part of a "community of the altar, under the sacred ministry of the bishop," has gathered; Christ is present, and the one, holy, catholic, and apostolic church is constituted.

> Carrying the Book of the Gospels slightly elevated,
> the deacon precedes the priest as he approaches
> the altar or else walks at the priest's side. (172)

For many centuries, long before the renewal of the diaconate as a permanent order, the deacon has been associated with the proclamation of the Gospel. At the deacon's ordination, the bishop presents the newly ordained deacon with the Book of the Gospels with the charge, "Receive the Gospel of Christ, whose herald you now are: Believe what you read, teach what you believe, and practice what you teach."[2] As will be seen in the next chapter on the Liturgy of the Word, it is the responsibility of the deacon to proclaim the Gospel; therefore, the option here for the deacon to be responsible for entering with the Book of the Gospels is ancient and most appropriate.

Notice that there is an option to be coordinated between the bishop or priest presiding and the deacon assisting at the Mass. If the deacon is carrying the Book of the Gospels, he processes ahead of the priest. If the Book of the

---

2. *Roman Pontifical.*

Gospels is not carried in procession, then the deacon simply walks next to the priest. If the deacon processes with the Book of the Gospels, of course, he should not do so while walking next to the priest!

Whether the deacon is carrying the Book of the Gospels or not determines his actions upon reaching the sanctuary. If he is not carrying the Book of the Gospels, the deacon enters the sanctuary with the priest, and together they reverence the altar with a profound bow and a kiss. If the deacon is carrying the Book of the Gospels, he omits the bow and proceeds directly to the altar and places the book upon it. He then awaits the priest and, together with him, kisses the altar.

The act of reverencing the altar with a kiss has a long and venerable history, one that is often misunderstood. Many older Catholics remember a time when an altar stone was imbedded within the altar itself, which contained a small relic of a saint (this practice is no longer required). Many Catholics thought that the kiss was being given to honor the saint whose relic was present, but this is not the case. The kiss is an act of reverence to the altar itself, which is a sign of Christ. An interesting parallel is found in the Byzantine tradition. A saint's relics are sewn into the *antimension*, a large rectangular cloth placed upon the altar. In fact, the *antimension* is in itself a kind of altar, and an Eastern Catholic priest may celebrate Divine Liturgy upon the *antimension* even if a consecrated altar is not available. However, while the Eastern Catholic priest kisses the altar, the Book of the Gospels, and the small hand cross at the beginning of the liturgy (while the deacon greets the altar with a kiss), the *antimension* is not similarly reverenced. The point here is that in both East and West reverence is being made to signs of Christ's presence, not to relics of saints. The altar itself represents Christ (and, in the Byzantine tradition, so do the Book of the Gospels and the hand cross); the clergy are greeting Christ when they enter the sanctuary and first approach the altar. That is why, even though in the Latin Church there is no longer a requirement to have an altar stone in the altar, and saints' relics are not present in every case, the act of kissing the altar remains.

The deacon assists the priest in preparing the thurible (sometimes referred to as the censer) if incense is used, and if desired the deacon may accompany the priest during the incensation. This is another area that requires prior coordination with the presider. Some prefer that the deacon walk next to him, holding the chasuble slightly away from the priest's arm to keep his vestments away from the hot censer. Other presiders just want the deacon to walk near him, but without handling the chasuble. Still others don't want the deacon anywhere in the vicinity! In this latter case, the deacon remains in a convenient location in the sanctuary to assist with the censer, if necessary, when the presider is finished with the incensation. Incensation is a powerful and ancient symbol associated with offering sacrifice to Almighty God. Consider Psalm 141: "Let my prayer be counted as incense before you, and the lifting up of my hands as an evening sacrifice." The deacon's role of assisting the presider at this point is quite meaningful: it expresses beautifully and simply the entire community's preparation for the sacrifice to come.

> After the incensation of the altar, [the deacon] goes to the chair together with the priest, takes his place there at the side of the priest and assists him as necessary....After the greeting of the people, the priest, the deacon, or a lay minister may very briefly introduce the faithful to the Mass of the day. (174, 50)

Notice that the deacon is seated at the side of the priest or bishop presiding at the Mass; this would also be the case in a concelebrated Mass. In this way the deacon is near the bishop or priest and physically able to assist him in any way necessary. This is worth mentioning since some liturgical planners, when dealing with the presence of concelebrants, tend to have all of the concelebrants sit together with the principal celebrant, with the deacon off to the side. However, this is not the way matters are described in the GIRM; the deacon is to "take his place at the side of the priest" to facilitate the presider's ministry as necessary.

The deacon is one of the ministers who may introduce the Mass; the GIRM indicates that this introduction is to be very brief. This is not the time for a mini homily or an introductory lecture or preliminary announcements.

The bishop or priest introduces the Penitential Rite, but the deacon, depending on the form of the Act of Penitence, may offer tropes or introduce the *Confiteor*. The GIRM also calls for a "brief pause for silence." As discussed earlier in the section on silence during the Mass, this shared responsibility between presider and deacon demands coordination. This is an opportunity for brief reflection by all in the assembly to call to mind their sins. Following the priest's introduction, the deacon does not rush into the next phase of the Act of Penitence, but allows a reasonable, but brief, period of silence.

Following the *Kyrie Eleison* and the *Gloria* (when used), the Introductory Rites culminate in the *Collect,* or Opening Prayer. The deacon's role is to assist as necessary with the Sacramentary; if his assistance is not needed, he simply joins with the entire assembly in prayer.

Conclusions

We have already seen the theological significance of the Introductory Rites in assembling the *communio* for worship. Within this diverse *communio* the deacon has a particular responsibility for the proclamation of the Gospel, and this is reflected in the option provided in the GIRM for the deacon to process into the assembly with the Book of the Gospels and to enthrone it on the altar.

Other responsibilities of the deacon during the Introductory Rites emphasize his servant role. He assists the bishop (or priest) with the incensation of the altar, he may assist as the liturgical options direct in the Act of Penitence, and he prays in silence along with the entire assembly as the priest offers the Collect, or Opening Prayer.

Questions for Reflection and Future Planning

1. How well is the gathering of the assembly understood as an integral part of the Mass itself? What practical steps might be taken to catechize parishes on the purpose of this part of the Mass?

2. Is there a preferred practice in your diocese or parish concerning whether the deacon carries the Book of the Gospels or walks next to the celebrant in the Entrance Procession? Are there ways in which the entrance of the Book of the Gospels might be linked to the Gospel Procession that takes place during the Liturgy of the Word?

3. What is the practice in your diocese or parish concerning the deacon's participation in the Act of Penitence?

CHAPTER THREE

Liturgy of the Word

===

Principles and Commentary

For easy reference, this chapter will begin with selected citations from the GIRM concerning the deacon's role at Mass. This is followed by commentary.

Text of the GIRM on the Liturgy of the Word

55. The main part of the Liturgy of the Word is made up of the readings from Sacred Scripture together with the chants occurring between them. The homily, Profession of Faith, and Prayer of the Faithful, however, develop and conclude this part of the Mass.

Silence
56. The Liturgy of the Word is to be celebrated in such a way as to promote meditation, and so any sort of haste that hinders recollection must clearly be avoided....It may be appropriate to observe such periods of silence, for example, before the Liturgy of the Word itself begins, after the first and second reading, and lastly at the conclusion of the homily.

Liturgy of the Word

The Biblical Readings

57. In the readings, the table of God's word is prepared for the faithful, and the riches of the Bible are opened to them.

58. In the celebration of the Mass with a congregation, the readings are always proclaimed from the ambo.

59. By tradition, the function of proclaiming the readings is ministerial, not presidential. The readings, therefore, should be proclaimed by a lector, and the Gospel by a deacon or, in his absence, a priest other than the celebrant. If, however, a deacon or another priest is not present, the priest celebrant himself should read the Gospel. Further, if another suitable lector is also not present, then the priest celebrant should also proclaim the other readings.

60. The reading of the Gospel is the high point of the Liturgy of the Word. The Liturgy itself teaches that great reverence is to be shown to it by setting it off from the other readings with special marks of honor: whether the minister appointed to proclaim it prepares himself by a blessing or prayer; or the faithful, standing as they listen to it being read, through their acclamations acknowledge and confess Christ present and speaking to them; or the very marks of reverence are given to the Book of the Gospels.

176. If, in addition, there is no other suitable lector present, the deacon should proclaim the other readings as well.

The Responsorial Psalm
61. After the first reading comes the responsorial Psalm, which is an integral part of the Liturgy of the Word and holds great liturgical and pastoral importance, because it fosters meditation on the word of God.

[The Acclamation Before the Gospel]
62. After the reading that immediately precedes the Gospel, the *Alleluia* or another chant indicated by the rubrics is sung, as required by the liturgical season. An acclamation of this kind constitutes a rite or act in itself, by which the assembly of the faithful welcomes and greets the Lord who is about to speak to them in the Gospel and professes their faith by means of the chant.

175. If incense is used, the deacon assists the priest when he puts incense in the thurible during the singing of the *Alleluia* or other chant. Then he makes a profound bow before the priest and asks for the blessing....Having bowed to the altar, he then takes up the *Book of the Gospels* which was placed upon it. He proceeds to the ambo, carrying the book slightly elevated. He is preceded by a thurifer, carrying a thurible with smoking incense, and by servers with lighted candles. There the deacon, with hands joined, greets the people, saying, "The Lord be with you." Then, at the words "A reading from the holy gospel according to...," he signs the book with his thumb and, afterwards, himself on his forehead, mouth, and breast. He

incenses the book and proclaims the Gospel reading. When the reading is concluded, he says the
acclamation, and all respond. He then venerates
the book with a kiss, saying privately, "May the
words of the gospel wipe out our offense," and
returns to the priest's side. When the deacon is
assisting the Bishop, he carries the book to him to
be kissed...In more solemn celebrations, as the
occasion suggests, a Bishop may impart a blessing
to the people with the Book of the Gospels. Lastly,
the deacon may carry the Book of the Gospels to
the credence table or to another appropriate and
dignified place.

The Homily
65. The homily is part of the Liturgy and is strongly
recommended, for it is necessary for the nurturing
of the Christian life. It should be an exposition of
some aspect of the readings from Sacred Scripture
or of another text from the Ordinary or from the
Proper of the Mass of the day and should take into
account both the mystery being celebrated and the
particular needs of the listeners.

66. The Homily should ordinarily be given by the
priest celebrant himself. He may entrust it to a concelebrating priest or occasionally, according to circumstances, to the deacon, but never to a lay person.
In particular cases and for a just cause, the homily
may even be given by a Bishop or a priest who is
present at the celebration but cannot concelebrate.

After the homily a brief period of silence is appropriately observed.

The Profession of Faith
67. The purpose of the *Symbolum* or Profession of Faith, or Creed, is that the whole gathered people may respond to the word of God proclaimed in the readings taken from Sacred Scripture and explained in the homily and that they may also call to mind and confess the great mysteries of the faith by reciting the rule of faith in a formula approved for liturgical use, before these mysteries are celebrated in the Eucharist.

68. The Creed is to be sung or said by the priest together with the people on Sundays and Solemnities. It may be said also at particular celebrations of a more solemn character.

The Prayer of the Faithful
69. In the Prayer of the Faithful, the people respond in a certain way to the word of God which they have welcomed in faith and, exercising the office of their baptismal priesthood, offer prayers to God for the salvation of all.

70. As a rule, the series of intentions is to be

   a. For the needs of the Church;
   b. For public authorities and the salvation of the whole world;
   c. For those burdened by any kind of difficulty;
   d. For the local community.

Nevertheless, in a particular celebration, such as Confirmation, Marriage, or a Funeral, the series of intentions may reflect more closely the particular occasion.

71. It is for the priest celebrant to direct this prayer from the chair. He himself begins it with a brief introduction, by which he invites the faithful to pray, and likewise he concludes it with a prayer. The intentions announced should be sober, be composed freely but prudently, and be succinct, and they should express the prayer of the entire community. The intentions are announced from the ambo or from another suitable place, by the deacon or by a cantor, a lector, or one of the lay faithful. The people, however, stand and give expression to their prayer either by an invocation said together after each intention or by praying in silence.

177. After the introduction by the priest it is the deacon himself who normally announces the intentions of the Prayer of the Faithful, from the ambo.

Commentary

The Liturgy of the Word consists of two major parts: first are the biblical readings themselves along with the chants associated with them; second are the homily, profession of faith, and the prayer of the faithful, which apply the readings to the life of the assembly. Through the Liturgy of the Word, "God speaks to his people, opening up to them the mystery of redemption and salvation, and offering them spiritual nourishment; and Christ himself is present in the midst of the faithful through his word" (GIRM 55).

GIRM 56 may seem almost ironic in calling for silence during proclamations of the scriptures, including responsorial psalms and other sung acclamations, preaching, and public prayer! Upon reflection, however, it is precisely *because* of all of this activity that silence takes on added significance. There is need to reflect upon the Word, to let it take root in the hearts and minds of the assembly. The deacon must understand the importance of this paragraph for many reasons. Chief among them, of course, is the simple fact that the deacon *must* have a deep understanding of *all* parts of the liturgy and its celebration. More directly, there is the very practical consideration that, as we will see shortly, the deacon may be called upon (in the absence of lectors) to proclaim the first and second readings in addition to the Gospel. The main goal of the Liturgy of the Word is captured well in this paragraph on silence: that "the word of God may be grasped by the heart and a response through prayer may be prepared."

Always proclaimed from the ambo when a congregation is present (58), the readings are a ministerial rather than presidential responsibility. In other words, *none* of the readings (including the Gospel) is the normal responsibility of the priest-celebrant. As GIRM 59 directs: "The readings, therefore, should be proclaimed by a lector, and the Gospel by a deacon." Note well that this is the *norm,* and the only time this may be set aside is in the absence of lectors or the deacon. With regard to the first and second readings, GIRM 176 directs that in the absence of lectors, "the deacon should proclaim the other readings as well." GIRM 59 further explains that in the absence of lectors or deacon, then the priest celebrant reads the first two readings.

GIRM 60 instructs that "the reading of the Gospel is the high point of the Liturgy of the Word." As we have seen, the deacon is the *ordinary* reader of the Gospel. According to GIRM 59, if a deacon is not present, then "in his absence" the Gospel may be read by "a priest other than the celebrant. If, however, a deacon or another priest is not present, the priest celebrant himself should read the Gospel." This passage is extremely important when examining the liturgical role of the deacon. It is not unusual for some priests to *insist* upon proclaiming the Gospel even when the deacon is present; as this paragraph emphatically demonstrates, *this should never be done*. It is *only* in the absence of a deacon that a priest other than the celebrant may read the Gospel (in a concelebrated Mass). Only in the absence of both the deacon and another priest may the priest-celebrant proclaim the Gospel. All of these directions serve to highlight the GIRM's insistence that the proclamation of the biblical readings is a *ministerial* rather than *presidential* function.

The ritual surrounding the proclamation of the Gospel may be found in GIRM 175. Even when incense is not used, the rest of the details still apply. While the full text is provided above, several points need to be highlighted. The deacon is to make a "profound bow" when asking the presider (priest or bishop) for the blessing before reading the Gospel. It is the practice in some locations for the deacon to kneel in front of the bishop when asking for the blessing. While this is not strictly called for by the GIRM, if kneeling is more convenient for the bishop and the deacon (and assuming the deacon has no physical impairment that would make kneeling and then standing impossible or impracticable), it may be acceptable. The deacon also bows to the altar, which is presumably between the presider and the ambo. Care should be taken to make this bow in a graceful and unhurried fashion. The movement from the chair to the ambo must reflect the solemn reverence being paid to the Gospel proclamation. This is true whether there is a solemn procession with acolytes and thurifer or the deacon is processing to the ambo alone.

Once at the ambo, the deacon is directed to greet the assembly with his hands joined. This is a bit counterintuitive, and many deacons (as well as many priests who proclaim the Gospel in the absence of the deacon) like to extend their arms outward toward the assembly as part of the greeting; technically, this ought *not* to be done. As with the solemn procession that precedes the Gospel, this greeting and the announcement of the Gospel passage to be proclaimed is a most solemn moment in the Liturgy of the Word. The greeting is not a personal greeting of the deacon to the assembly; rather, it is the beginning of a formal proclamation and should be given the gravitas it merits. This solemnity extends to the announcement of the Gospel passage; this is not being offered to the assembly so they can find the passage in their missalettes! Rather, this is also part of the solemn proclamation. This is why the incensation, when used, follows the solemn invocation of greeting and announcement. Everything that precedes the actual proclamation of the words of the Gospel—the sung acclamation, the blessing and prayer of the proclaimer, the procession to the ambo, the greeting and announcement, the incensation—serves to underscore the significance and centrality of Christ's presence in the proclamation of the Gospel itself.

Following the proclamation, the norm is for the deacon to reverence the Book of the Gospels with a kiss, while saying silently the traditional prayer, "May the words of the Gospel wipe away our sins." When assisting a bishop, however, the deacon should inquire in advance about the bishop's preferences with regard to kissing the Book of the Gospels following the proclamation and follow the bishop's direction.

We now come to the homily. According to canon 764:

> Without prejudice to the prescript of c. 765, presbyters and deacons possess the faculty of preaching everywhere; this faculty is to be exercised with at least the presumed consent of the rector of the church, unless the competent ordinary has restricted or taken away the faculty or particular law requires express permission.

The deacon, according to GIRM 65 and 94, preaches the homily at Mass "occasionally" or "from time to time." The Latin text in both paragraphs is *quandoque*, and either

English translation is acceptable, although the word also conveys a sense of some frequency. One set of definitions, for example, includes "whenever," "whensoever," and "as often as"![1] The most fundamental point involved is that the deacon, as an ordained minister of the Word, shares in the responsibility for offering a homily during the Eucharist. According to GIRM 65, the homily "should be an exposition of some aspect of the readings from Sacred Scripture or of another text from the Ordinary or from the Proper of the Mass of the day and should take into account both the mystery being celebrated and the particular needs of the listeners." GIRM 66 prefers that the homily be given by the priest celebrant, and that he may "occasionally, according to circumstances" entrust it to the deacon. "Occasionally" means just that—on occasion. Some have interpreted this to mean that the deacon should not be "scheduled" to preach with regularity, but this seems to read too much into the norm. The *Vatican Directory*, citing canon 764, states that "it is for the deacon to proclaim the Gospel and preach the word of God. Deacons have the faculty to preach everywhere, in accordance with the conditions established by law. This faculty is founded on the Sacrament of Ordination and should be exercised with at least the tacit consent of the rector of the churches concerned...."[2] Through ordination, the deacon shares in the *primum officium* of the bishop, to be exercised in communion with the

---

1. *A Latin Dictionary*, (New York: Oxford University Press, 1987), 1505.
2. *Vatican Directory*, 24.

presbyters. A particularly interesting insight from the history of the renewal of the diaconate is germane.

As early as 1840 in Germany, interest in the possibility of a renewed diaconate in the Latin Church may be found.[3] Even in these early days, official preaching and teaching in the name of the bishop was envisioned. During the antepreparatory phase of the Second Vatican Council, 101 specific proposals were made concerning the possible renewal of a permanent diaconate. Sixteen of these proposals, representing the input of seventy-one bishops, addressed possible functions to be exercised by such deacons in the future.[4] The majority of these functions related to the deacon's role in overall catechesis and religious education, with several of them particularly focused on the function of preaching at Mass. Throughout the century in which the possibilities of a renewed diaconate developed, especially in Germany, there was a solid expectation that the deacon would be an ordinary minister of preaching at Mass.

Clearly, balance and prudence must be sought here. Priests, of course, preside over the Eucharist and have a normative responsibility for the homily at Mass. Nonetheless, although deacons do not preside at the Mass, they too are ordained to a participation in the bishop's ministry, which

---

3. See, for example, Josef Hornef, "The Genesis and Growth of the Proposal," in *Foundations for the Renewal of the Diaconate* (Washington, DC: United States Catholic Conference, 1993), 6.

4. *Acta et documenta Concilio oecuminco Vaticano II apparando; Series prima (antepraeparatoria)* (Typis Polyglottis Vaticanis, 1960–61), II/II, 128–31.

includes a share in the *primum officium* of preaching. Deacons are authorized to give homilies by canon law (764) and the expectations of their bishops. Although the GIRM refers to deacons preaching "occasionally," this should not be interpreted as meaning "extraordinarily." The deacon has an *ordinary* responsibility to preach at Mass, and unless his bishop decides to restrict this general faculty given in the universal law, he is obliged to exercise that ministry with some regularity. As with most things, therefore, wisdom stands in the middle: while deacons should not preach exclusively, neither should they never preach.

Another problem area needs to be mentioned. In some locations, deacons *only* assist at Mass when they are scheduled to preach; they do not assist at Mass when they are *not* preaching. This practice of *exclusively* linking assistance at Mass with preaching is very problematic. Preaching and assisting at Mass, while certainly related, are not inherently linked, and the sacramental sign of the deacon serving at Mass, even when not preaching, needs to be given full value.

To summarize, then, the intent of canon law, the Rite of Ordination of Deacons, and the GIRM: *the deacon is to preach liturgically.* The pastoral question becomes, With what frequency and under what conditions will the deacon exercise this ordinary function? This should be a matter of reflection and discussion for priests, deacons, and liturgical planners.

After the homily and a brief period of silence, and after the Profession of Faith, the assembly moves on to the Prayer of the Faithful. GIRM 69–71 provides that the Prayer of the

Faithful be included in Masses with a congregation, and that the intentions "as a rule" are for the needs of the church, for public authorities "and the salvation of the whole world," for those in need, and for the local community. Certain celebrations may suggest additional intentions.

The priest celebrant introduces and concludes the intentions with a prayer. The intentions, however, are offered by other ministers; GIRM 71 specifies "the deacon, a cantor, a lector, or one of the lay faithful." GIRM 177 directs more specifically that "after the introduction by the priest it is the deacon himself who *normally* announces the intentions of the Prayer of the Faithful, from the ambo" (emphasis added). This seems to give a particular emphasis to the role of the deacon in this regard. It is the deacon who, in very practical terms, should know the concerns of the local church and be able to bring these concerns to the assembly's prayer. It is natural to expect that the deacon, who should be providing parish leadership in meeting the needs of others, be the one to articulate these needs publicly.

Two cautionary notes: First, any minister involved in the preparation of the General Intercessions must keep in mind the overall themes to be covered, as outlined in GIRM 70: for the needs of the Church, for public authorities and the world's salvation, for those burdened by any affliction, and for the local community. Although adaptation is certainly encouraged for certain celebrations, it is appropriate to keep this general framework in mind. Second, the General Intercessions are to be prayers of intercession on behalf of the people of God, not a listing of prayers for individuals, nor are they to be prayers of thanksgiving for blessings received. So, while we all want to pray that Aunt Sadie will get over her illness, we do so in the context of praying that all of those who are ill in our community will find healing: this is what makes the intercessions "general," as opposed to with particular. It is yet another sign that Mass is an act of the *communio discipulorum,* an act of the assembled community-qua-community, not a gathering of individuals who just happen to be praying together at the same time.

Conclusions

The deacon is ordained to a ministry of Word, sacrament, and charity. Because of this ordination, the deacon participates in an ordinary way as a minister of the Word, especially of the Gospel. Recalling some of the theological themes discussed earlier in the introduction of this book, we find a particular resonance here. It is properly the role of the deacon to proclaim the Gospel, not merely because of the deacon's longstanding traditional association with the Gospel, but because the deacon, by virtue of ordination, is a sacramental model that exists in the "between" of the Gospel proclaimed and the Gospel lived: the link between Eucharist and justice.

The deacon's preaching should also have a uniquely diaconal character. The deacon's homilies should be particularly prophetic, calling the people to be true to the diaconal responsibility of initiation, to take the Gospel out of the assembly and into the world at large. Deacons can bring to their preaching the perspectives of living, working, and ministering "in the world," and the impact of the Good News of Christ. In a church charged to read "the signs of the times in the light of the Gospel" (*Gaudium et specs* 4), deacons may offer valuable reflections to the church.

The deacon's role during the Liturgy of the Word takes on a different character from the Introductory Rites. While primarily an assistant to the presider during the Introductory Rites (with perhaps the most notable exception being the option of the deacon carrying the Book of the Gospels during the entrance procession), he is clearly a servant of the Word during the Liturgy of the Word. Here his service is directed toward the assembly itself: proclaiming the Gospel, preaching occasionally, and offering the General Intercessions.

Questions for Reflection and Future Planning

1. In your experience, when deacons are present and assisting at Mass, do they proclaim the Gospel? If not, why not?

2. What is the approach taken to deacons preaching in your parish or diocese?

3. When deacons preach, is there a discernible diaconal quality to their preaching?

4. Who offers the intentions of the Prayer of the Faithful in your parish? Do deacons participate in the preparation and offering of these intentions?

CHAPTER FOUR

Liturgy of the Eucharist

Principles and Commentary

For easy reference, this chapter will begin with selected citations from the GIRM concerning the deacon's role at Mass. This is followed by commentary.

Text of the GIRM on the Liturgy of the Eucharist

72. At the Last Supper Christ instituted the Paschal Sacrifice and banquet by which the Sacrifice of the Cross is continuously made present in the Church whenever the priest, representing Christ the Lord, carries out what the Lord himself did and handed over to his disciples to be done in his memory.

The Preparation of the Gifts

73. At the beginning of the Liturgy of the Eucharist the gifts, which will become Christ's Body and Blood, are brought to the altar.

First, the altar, the Lord's table, which is the center of the whole Liturgy of the Eucharist, is prepared by placing on it the corporal, purificator,

Missal, and chalice (unless the chalice is prepared at the credence table).

The offerings are then brought forward. It is praiseworthy for the bread and wine to be presented by the faithful. They are then accepted at an appropriate place by the priest or the deacon and carried to the altar.

75. The bread and wine are placed on the altar by the priest to the accompaniment of the prescribed formulas. The priest may incense the gifts placed upon the altar and then incense the cross and the altar itself, so as to signify the Church's offering and prayer rising like incense in the sight of God. Next, the priest, because of his sacred ministry, and the people, by reason of their baptismal dignity, may be incensed by the deacon or another minister.

178. After the Prayer of the Faithful, while the priest remains at the chair, the deacon prepares the altar, assisted by the acolyte, but it is the deacon's place to take care of the sacred vessels himself. He also assists the priest in receiving the people's gifts. Next, he hands the priest the paten with the bread to be consecrated, pours wine and a little water into the chalice, saying quietly,...*By the mystery of this water,* and after this presents the chalice to the priest. He may also carry out the preparation of the chalice at the credence table. If incense is used, the deacon assists the priest during the incensation

of the gifts, the cross, and the altar; afterwards, the deacon himself or the acolyte incenses the priest and the people.

The Prayer Over the Offerings
The Eucharistic Prayer
78. Now the center and summit of the entire celebration begins: namely, the Eucharistic Prayer, that is, the prayer of thanksgiving and sanctification.

179. During the Eucharistic Prayer, the deacon stands near the priest but slightly behind him, so that when needed he may assist the priest with the chalice or the Missal.

From the epiclesis until the priest shows the chalice, the deacon normally remains kneeling. If several deacons are present, one of them may place incense in the thurible for the consecration and incense the host and the chalice as they are shown to the people.

215. After the prayer over the offerings has been said by the principal celebrant, the concelebrants approach the altar and stand around it, but in such a way that they do not obstruct the execution of the rites and that the sacred action may be seen clearly by the faithful. They should not be in the deacon's way whenever he needs to go to the altar to perform his ministry.

The deacon exercises his ministry at the altar whenever he needs to assist with the chalice and the Missal. However, insofar as possible, he stands back slightly, behind the concelebrating priests standing around the principal celebrant.

The Communion Rite

The Lord's Prayer

The Rite of Peace
181. After the priest has said the prayer at the Rite of Peace and the greeting…, the deacon, if it is appropriate, invites all to exchange the sign of peace. He faces the people and, with hands joined, says, "Let us offer each other the sign of peace." Then he himself receives the sign of peace from the priest and may offer it to those other ministers who are closer to him.

239. After the deacon or, when no deacon is present, one of the concelebrants has said the invitation…*Let us offer each other the sign of peace,* all exchange the sign of peace with one another. The concelebrants who are nearer the principal celebrant receive the sign of peace from him before the deacon does.

The Fraction
83. The priest breaks the Eucharistic Bread, assisted, if the case calls for it, by the deacon or a concelebrant….The fraction or breaking of bread is begun after the sign of peace and is carried out with proper reverence, though it should not be unnecessarily prolonged, nor should it be accorded

undue importance. This rite is reserved to the priest and the deacon.

240. While the *Agnus Dei* is sung or said, the deacons or some of the concelebrants may help the principal celebrant break the hosts for Communion, both of the concelebrants and of the people.

Communion

182. After the priest's Communion, the deacon receives Communion under both kinds from the priest himself and then assists the priest in distributing Communion to the people. If Communion is given under both kinds, the deacon himself administers the chalice to the communicants; and, when the distribution is completed, he immediately and reverently consumes at the altar all of the Blood of Christ that remains, assisted if necessary by other deacons and priests.

183. When the distribution of Communion is completed, the deacon returns to the altar with the priest and collects the fragments, if any remain, and then carries the chalice and other sacred vessels to the credence table, where he purifies them and arranges them in the usual way while the priest returns to the chair. It is also permissible to leave the vessels that need to be purified, suitably covered, at the credence table on a corporal and to purify them immediately after Mass following the dismissal of the people.

244. [During Masses with concelebrants,] the con-celebrants do likewise [reverently consume the Body and Blood of Christ], communicating them-selves. After them the deacon receives the Body and Blood of the Lord from the principal celebrant.

247. The deacon reverently drinks at the altar all of the Blood of Christ that remains, assisted, if neces-sary, by some of the concelebrants. He then carries the chalice over to the credence table and there he or a duly instituted acolyte purifies, wipes, and arranges it in the usual way (cf. above, no. 183).

284. When Communion is distributed under both kinds,

  a. The chalice is usually administered by a dea-con or, when no deacon is present, by a priest, or even by a duly instituted acolyte or another extraordinary minister of Holy Communion, or by a member of the faithful who in case of necessity has been entrusted with this duty for a single occasion;
  b. Whatever may remain of the Blood of Christ is consumed at the altar by the priest or the deacon or the duly instituted acolyte who ministered the chalice. The same then puri-fies, wipes, and arranges the sacred vessels in the usual way.

    Any of the faithful who wish to receive Holy Communion under the species of bread alone should be granted their wish.

Commentary

GIRM 72 observes that the church has arranged the Liturgy of the Eucharist "in parts corresponding to the words and actions of Christ." First, the Preparation of the Gifts involves bread and wine, "the same elements which Christ took into his hands." Then the Eucharistic Prayer gives thanks to God "for the whole work of salvation," and the elements are transformed into the Body and Blood of Christ. Through the fraction and communion, the entire assembly receives from "the one bread the Lord's Body and from the one cup the Lord's Blood." The primary role of the deacon throughout the Liturgy of the Eucharist is one of service and assistance.

Following the Prayer of the Faithful, the altar is prepared for the Liturgy of the Eucharist. "While the priest remains at the chair, the deacon prepares the altar, assisted by the acolyte, but it is the deacon's place to take care of the sacred vessels himself" (178). According to GIRM 73, the altar is prepared "by placing on it the corporal, purificator, Missal, and chalice (unless the chalice is prepared at the credence table)." Deacons must be sensitive to the customs of the location in which they are serving. In many places, the preparation of the altar is assigned to other ministers, such as altar servers. The deacon works collaboratively with these ministers; nonetheless, the deacon has a particular responsibility, according to the GIRM, for the vessels that will contain the Body and Blood of the Lord: paten, chalice, and ciborium.

The gifts are presented and received by the priest or deacon (73, 178). At the altar, the deacon "hands the priest the paten with the bread to be consecrated, pours wine and a little water into the chalice," saying quietly the prescribed prayer (178). As I observed in the introduction, the beautiful prayer that accompanies this action is one of the most theologically rich statements of the entire Mass: "By the mystery of this water and wine, may we come to share in the divinity of Christ, who humbled himself to share in our humanity." It states simply the kenotic action of Christ ("who humbled himself to share in our humanity") and the theotic goal that results ("may we come to share in the divinity of Christ").[1] Nonetheless, it is to be said in a low voice, and not be given prominence. The act of adding the water to the wine, while theologically significant, is nonetheless a preliminary act of preparation of the wine, and the prayer should not rival the other prayers being offered at this point in the liturgy.

Before leaving the subject of adding a little water to the wine, a practical point needs to be made. In most pastoral situations, more than one chalice is necessary to accommodate the number of communicants. Current practice is to prepare these multiple cups prior to the beginning of Mass and bring them to the altar during the Preparation of the Gifts. Alternatively, these cups may be prepared at the altar

---

1. See William T. Ditewig, "The Kenotic Leadership of Deacons," in James Keating, ed., *The Deacon Reader: New Issues and Cross-Currents in the Diaconate* (Mahwah, NJ: Paulist Press, 2006), 248-277.

during the same period. Especially in large communities, this process can be quite challenging. The challenge is made worse by a deacon who attempts to place a little water in each and every cup!

Pouring wine "and a little water" in the chalice is a liturgical act, not a chemical one. By this I mean simply that it is not necessary to add water to each and every cup that is to be used; rather, a little water may be added to the principal chalice only, which is then handed to the presider. Depending on pastoral circumstances, the options seem to be these: (1) if all of the cups are prepared *before* Mass begins and brought to the altar during the Preparation of the Gifts, the principal chalice should still be prepared immediately prior to handing it to the priest so that the action of pouring the wine and adding the water to that chalice is visible to the assembly; (2) if a large vessel is used to contain the wine that will subsequently be poured out into smaller vessels for communion, it is possible to add the water to the wine in the larger vessel. I am stressing two points: the action of pouring the wine, adding a little water, and handing the principal chalice to the presider should all be clearly visible to the assembly so that the sign value of the action may be received. Second, it is not necessary to add the water to each vessel, especially if this would unduly extend the time given to the action. Liturgically, we need to focus attention on "one bread," which will later be broken, and "one cup," which will later be shared; actions that distract from this focus should be minimized. I once assisted at a Mass celebrated in

a most historic basilica. There were many people at the celebration, with a cardinal serving as principal celebrant and
many bishops and priests as concelebrants. We prepared
dozens of cups before Mass, and during the Preparation of
the Gifts, they were brought two by two to the deacon at the
altar. Once all the cups were in place, the principal chalice
was brought to the altar, where I added wine and a little
water before handing it to the cardinal. In my opinion, it is
most important to draw the focus of the assembly to the
principal chalice being used by the presider.

If incense is used, the deacon assists the priest with the
incensation of the gifts, the cross, and the altar; and then
incenses the priest, concelebrants, and the people (75, 178).
The deacon's duties during this process require him to be
constantly aware of the rhythm and pace of the liturgy. He
needs to move *seamlessly and gracefully* between handling,
preparing, and presenting the gifts; assisting the priest with
the incensation of the gifts and cross; and shifting his focus
to concelebrants (if any) and the people, and then back to
the priest-celebrant at the altar. All of this comes together in
the Prayer Over the Offerings, after which the Eucharistic
Prayer begins.

During the Eucharistic Prayer, "the deacon stands near
the priest but slightly behind him, so that when needed he
may assist the priest with the chalice or the Missal" (179).
This includes concelebrated Masses, in which the concelebrants gather around the altar. GIRM 215 reminds concelebrants that they should "not obstruct the execution of the

rites and that the sacred action may be seen clearly by the faithful. They should not be in the deacon's way whenever he needs to go to the altar to perform his ministry." According to the GIRM, the deacon is to "stand back slightly, behind the concelebrating priests," and move forward to assist whenever necessary with the chalice and the Missal. Once again, the deacon's own awareness of what is happening around him will be critical. Without drawing the focus of the people to himself, the deacon must nonetheless be assertive enough to move gracefully between assisting with the book or chalice as necessary, and returning into the background to keep the focus of attention on the priest and the Eucharistic action.

From the *epiclesis* before the consecration until the showing of the chalice immediately after the consecration, the deacon "normally" remains kneeling (77). While this action is *normative,* it is not *absolute.* In other words, while kneeling is preferred, there can be many legitimate reasons for the deacon *not* to kneel at this point. The point behind kneeling is, of course, to show reverence for the action taking place at the altar; it is designed to help the assembly focus its full attention on the consecration. Therefore, any action of the deacon that might serve to distract that attention must be avoided. If, for example, the deacon is physically incapable of kneeling and rising with some degree of grace, his actions will serve to draw attention to himself and away from the Eucharistic action. In short, deciding whether to kneel or not will require coordination with the bishop or priest celebrating the Mass, as well as a pastoral sensitivity to the particular situation of the minister involved, and a dose of common sense.

Priests and deacons should also be clear about the period of time involved in this action. The deacon, if he is going to kneel, should do so, *not* from the beginning of the Eucharistic Prayer, but from the *epiclesis* (although in some forms of the Eucharistic Prayer the *epiclesis* takes place near the beginning of the Prayer). The deacon is to return to his feet after the showing of the chalice at the consecration; however, some have misunderstood this to mean the elevation of the gifts during the *Per ipsum* ("Through Him, with Him, and in Him...."), which concludes the Eucharistic Prayer.

I must share a true story. I once received a phone call from a pastor who was concerned over this point. A newly ordained priest had been assigned to the parish, and the pastor had asked the deacon to assist the new priest at Mass as much as possible. One day the pastor was passing by the church during Mass, and he stopped by to observe how things were going. He noticed that at the *epiclesis* the deacon knelt down and therefore disappeared from the pastor's view. This was a new practice, and the pastor was interested to see what would happen next. The priest continued with the Eucharistic Prayer. Following the consecration, the priest showed the host to the assembly, and then the chalice. The deacon remained out of view, still kneeling. However, as soon as the priest replaced the chalice onto the altar, the deacon's hand appeared, replaced the pall on the chalice, and then disappeared again. The deacon remained kneeling until the *Per ipsum,* when he struggled to his feet and elevated the chalice as normal. The pastor wanted to know if this was what the GIRM intends. It most assuredly is not!

Returning to the actions of the deacon at the consecration:

Another option described in GIRM 179 is that, if several deacons are assisting, "one of them may place incense in the thurible for the consecration and incense the host and the chalice as they are shown to the people." While this option is no longer exercised as frequently as it used to be, deacons and other pastoral ministers need to be aware of its existence.

It has mistakenly been thought in some places that the Memorial Acclamation ("Let us proclaim the Mystery of Faith") was the proper responsibility of the deacon; it is not.[2] Although in structure it may seem similar to other hortative lines of the deacon (such as "Let us offer each other the sign of peace"), the Memorial Acclamation is a part of the Eucharistic Prayer itself and is reserved to the principal celebrant.

Finally, at the concluding doxology, "the deacon stands next to the priest, holding the chalice elevated while the priest elevates the paten with the host, until the people have responded with the acclamation, *Amen*" (180). *Only* the priest says or chants the concluding doxology; the deacon

---

2. This error was even contained in a text from the National Conference of Catholic Bishops (now the United States Conference of Catholic Bishops), *Deacon: Minister of Word and Sacrament: Study Text VI* (Washington, DC: United States Catholic Conference, 1979). While this text has not been approved for use for many years, it had considerable influence in the liturgical formation of deacons.

assists him in silence until he joins together with the entire assembly in the great "Amen" that concludes the Eucharistic Prayer. In addition, only the celebrant and the deacon elevate the consecrated elements. During concelebrated Masses, the principal celebrant does not distribute other vessels to concelebrants for elevation. The intent of the elevation is to highlight the One Bread (elevated by the priest) and the One Cup (elevated by the deacon) as an act of offering ourselves and our sacrifice "through Him, with Him, and in Him."

Following the Eucharistic Prayer, the focus of the liturgy shifts to actions intended to help the assembly be properly disposed to receive communion. "This is the sense of the fraction and the other preparatory rites by which the faithful are led directly to Communion" (80). This, then, is the goal of the deacon: to exercise his role with the intent of preparing the assembly to receive communion.

After the Lord's Prayer, the Rite of Peace takes place. The priest says the prayer, and then extends the greeting of peace to the whole assembly. The deacon, "if it is appropriate," invites all to exchange the sign of peace (181). The question of appropriateness has to do with whether the greeting of peace will be extended at all, not whether it should be the deacon who invites the assembly to exchange the sign of peace. As mentioned above, the deacon will need to come forward, sometimes through a sea of concelebrants, to extend this invitation. He should not attempt to shout it out from behind the concelebrants, nor should he simply eliminate it. Concelebrants, again, need to be reminded to be aware of the deacon's role and to be prepared to give him the space in which to exercise it.

The particular sign of peace may be established by the bishops' conference. "It is, however, appropriate that each person offer the sign of peace only to those who are nearest and in a sober manner" (82). The intent of this instruction is twofold: to prevent the exchange of peace from being unduly prolonged, thus disturbing the normal pace of the liturgy, and also to discourage forms of the exchange of peace that may be overly exuberant and inappropriate to the serious intent of the Rite itself and the Mass in general. In concelebrated Masses, "the concelebrants who are nearer the principal celebrant receive the sign of peace from him before the deacon does" (239). Here again, common sense should prevail: it is likely that concelebrants will be physically closer to the principal celebrant; it makes perfect sense that they would exchange the sign of peace first.

The fraction rite recalls Christ's action of breaking the bread at the Last Supper. It "signifies that the many faithful are made one body (1 Cor 10:17) by receiving Communion from the one Bread of Life which is Christ, who died and rose for the salvation of the world." The deacon may assist in the fraction, as may concelebrants, if present (83, 240). While the faction is to be done reverently, "it should not be unnecessarily prolonged, nor should it be accorded undue importance" (83).

The deacon receives communion under both kinds from the priest celebrant; he then assists the priest and other ministers in distributing communion to the assembly. At concelebrated Masses, the deacon receives communion from the principal celebrant after the other concelebrants have received (244). Most deacons, however, learn to be quite flexible at this point in the Mass, since actual practice varies widely among presiders.

Traditionally, the deacon has been associated with the chalice, and for that reason, the deacon often administers the chalice to the people. The language of the GIRM, however, does not *restrict* the deacon to ministering the chalice. As circumstances require, the deacon—as an ordinary minister of communion—may distribute either species as necessary. After communion, "he immediately and reverently consumes at the altar all of the Blood of Christ that remains, assisted if necessary by other deacons and priests" (182, 247). The deacon also collects any fragments that remain and carries the chalice and other vessels to the credence table.

> He purifies them and arranges them in the usual way while the priest returns to the chair. It is also permissible to leave the vessels that need to be purified, suitably covered, at the credence table on a corporal and to purify them immediately after Mass following the dismissal of the people. (183)

After the distribution of communion, and after the sacred vessels have been properly cared for, the Rite of Communion comes to an end with the Prayer after Communion. Despite occasional practice to the contrary, announcements are not made prior to this Prayer. The time after reception of communion is an opportunity for prayer and reflection, and this period extends until the celebrant brings it to a close with the Prayer after Communion.

Conclusions

The role of the deacon during the Liturgy of the Eucharist consists of several shifts of focus. During the Eucharistic Prayer itself, the deacon's focus is on the altar and the celebrant, ensuring that everything is in order and that the celebrant can exercise his own role with reverence, grace, and dignity. After the concluding doxology, the focus shifts to preparing the entire assembly for communion. This includes the invitation to extend the sign of peace, assisting with the fraction rite, and distributing communion (especially the Precious Blood, if communion is offered under both forms). Following communion, the deacon's focus shifts to the suitable purification of the sacred vessels (or preparing them for later purification immediately after Mass), and preparing the altar and sanctuary for the Concluding Rites to follow.

Through all of this, the deacon should be attentive, alert, and sensitive to the pastoral situation around him. In all of his movements, gestures, and actions throughout the Mass, he must act with a measured reverence and grace to do what needs to be done, but without drawing undue attention to himself as he does so (except, obviously, when he is addressing the assembly). This demands good formation and considerable practice, in addition to knowing the particular expectations and demands of the local church.

Questions for Reflection and Future Planning

1. What is the current practice in your own parish for receiving the gifts of the assembly? Do deacons assist in this act?

2. How is the preparation of the altar being accomplished at this time? Are deacons involved?

3. Who invites the assembly at the Memorial Acclamation ("Let us proclaim the Mystery of Faith")?

CHAPTER FIVE

Concluding Rites

====

Principles and Commentary

For easy reference, this chapter will begin with selected citations from the GIRM concerning the deacon's role at the Mass. This is followed by commentary.

Text of the GIRM on the Concluding Rites

[Announcements]
184. Once the prayer after Communion has been said, the deacon makes brief announcements to the people, if indeed any need to be made, unless the priest prefers to do this himself.

[Greeting and Blessing]
185. [First comes the greeting and the response: *The Lord be with you.* Then] if a prayer over the people or a solemn formula for the blessing is used, the deacon says,...*Bow your heads and pray for God's blessing.*

[Dismissal]
185. After the priest's blessing, the deacon, with hands joined and facing the people, dismisses them, saying,...*The Mass is ended, go in peace.*

[Departure of the Ministers]
186. Then, together with the priest, the deacon venerates the altar with a kiss, makes a profound bow, and departs in a manner similar to the procession beforehand.

Commentary

The Concluding Rites are brief and not unduly extended. Just as the Introductory Rites serve to help the assembly celebrate its ecclesial identity as it gives thanks to God through Word and sacrament, the Concluding Rites help the church carry the effects of its worship into the world.

As mentioned in the last chapter, the announcements are made only *after* the Prayer after Communion, which closes the Rite of Communion. The GIRM's direction also implies that only those announcements that must be made should be made. Again, the point is that the Concluding Rites are not to be excessively long. If announcements need to be made because it was impracticable to include them in the parish bulletin, they should be brief and to the point. Announcements should not be made from the ambo, which is the privileged location for the proclamation of sacred scripture. The deacon, because of his unique servant relationship to the assembly, is the normal minister to make the announcements, although the priest may elect to make them himself.

While GIRM 185 offers only one English formula for the dismissal, the Missal itself offers several, and the deacon may choose any of them. He may not, however, offer some form of extended commentary or minihomily. The purpose of the dismissal is more than a simple "adjournment" of the Mass. Rather its purpose is well-expressed in GIRM 90: "so that each may go out to do good works, praising and blessing God."

It may reasonably be asked why the deacon, and not the priest-celebrant who has presided over the Eucharistic Celebration, should be the minister to dismiss the assembly. Without overemphasizing the point, it might be said that the deacon is the normal minister for the dismissal because it is the deacon who is the sacramental sign of the church's own diaconal nature in the world. In a real sense, the deacon is dismissing the assembly to go out into the world and to live out the implications of the Eucharist that has been celebrated. Once again the deacon may be seen as the sacramental model that is the link between the Eucharist and justice.

After the dismissal, the deacon processes out at the side of the priest, carrying nothing. If the deacon entered carrying the Book of the Gospels, of course, he does *not* do so now. When a bishop is the principal celebrant, the deacon walks a little ahead of or behind the bishop during the procession. This is done so the bishop may have sufficient freedom of movement to bless the assembly as he departs. The bishop's preference should be sought before Mass begins.

Questions for Reflection and Future Planning

1. How are announcements handled in your parish? Are they brief and necessary? Who makes them?

2. How effectively do the Concluding Rites as celebrated in your parish help the assembly transition from the Eucharistic Celebration to the demands of Christian discipleship "in the world"?

CONCLUDING REFLECTION

The Deacon in the Sacred Liturgy

This brief reflection on the deacon's liturgical role in the Mass, based on the current *General Instruction of the Roman Missal,* has tried to situate this role within the larger framework of the deacon's sacramental identity and three-fold ministry of Word, sacrament, and servant-leadership. The Eucharist is the central act of our lives as Catholic Christians, an act in which Christ continues to constitute the church herself.

Through sacramental ordination, the deacon is configured in a special way to Christ, who came not to be served, but to serve. Christ, through his total self-emptying *(kenosis)* and ultimate glorification, effects the salvation of all who follow him on the path of the discipleship. The deacon, then, is a sacramental sign of the kenotic Christ, and this sacramental identity is exercised through his threefold ministry. In the Eucharist, the defining "source and summit" of the church, all dimensions of the deacon's identity find expression.

As minister of the Word, the deacon has a special responsibility for bearing the Gospel into the assembly and proclaiming the Gospel to all. In this ministry, he acts *in persona Christi,* since it is Christ's own Gospel, and ultimately Christ himself who proclaims that Gospel. The deacon also preaches the Good News, helping to explain and apply the implications of the Gospel to the lives of the assembly. In the name of the community, he gives voice to their needs and places those needs before God in prayer. As minister of sacrament, the deacon is an ordinary minister of communion, especially the Precious Blood, which was poured out for our salvation: another sign of the kenotic Christ. Traditionally, the deacon has had a special responsibility for the Precious Blood, reflected in the current liturgy by his elevation of the chalice at the concluding doxology and his distribution of the Precious Blood at communion. As minister of charity and justice, the deacon serves the bishop and his priests throughout the liturgy, exhorts the people to prayer, and dismisses the assembly to live out the demands of discipleship in the world.

It has been said that the Second Vatican Council did not restore the diaconate because of a shortage of priests, but because of a shortage of deacons. This statement captures a most significant insight: the diaconate is not needed for the uniqueness of its particular functions; in fact, the deacon shares most of his functions with others. Rather, the council was signaling that what was needed was a new way of "doing ministry," a way that sacramentalizes the very servant-nature of the church, much as the ministerial priesthood of bishops and priests sacramentalizes the priestly nature of the Church.

The Deacon at Mass

For well over a millennium, the diaconate was experienced as a transitional state leading ultimately to the priesthood. As such, it was described and defined by the "end" of the sacrament, which was the priesthood. The Second Vatican Council changed that perspective when it renewed the permanent diaconate. Now the diaconate must be seen, understood, experienced, and expressed in terms that are no longer priestly, but diaconal. This presents theologians and all pastoral ministers wonderful opportunities. In terms of the liturgical role of the deacon at Mass, it means that the deacon's actions must be understood, not as acts of "priests, junior grade" (to use the expression of theologian Richard Gaillardetz), but in their uniquely diaconal thrust.

This guide is a modest attempt—and perhaps a pastoral challenge —to understand the deacon's role in this new light.

Liturgical Vestments of the Deacon

―――――

in the order worn

Amice (optional). Usually, a white linen rectangle worn over the cleric's shoulders. Originally a kind of hood, its purpose today is to cover the cleric's street clothes at the neck. According to the GIRM, it is an optional vestment, which is unnecessary if the alb used is designed to completely cover the cleric's street clothes.

Alb. A long, white gown common to all liturgical ministers. It is one of the most ancient of all vestments, and it is worn under all other vestments (except for the amice, if used). The alb is white because it signifies the white garment given to the newly baptized during the rite of baptism.

Cincture (optional). A cord used to serve as a belt around the alb. It is sometimes used to hold the cleric's stole in place. The cincture is optional depending on the style of alb used.

Stole. A narrow strip of cloth, in the appropriate liturgical colors matching the dalmatic and chasuble, that signifies a cleric's order (bishop, priest, deacon). Deacons wear the stole over the left shoulder, diagonally across the chest, and secured at the right hip. One reason offered for this style of wear is that it keeps the deacon's right hand and arm free for service.

Dalmatic. The outer liturgical vestment of the deacon at Mass. It is a knee-length, sleeved garment in the appropriate liturgical color. The dalmatic is to the deacon what the chasuble is to the priest, and it is to be worn whenever a priest would wear the chasuble. Originally a garment from Dalmatia, it is the sign of the servant. The dalmatic was originally a vestment of the bishop, and bishops continue to wear the dalmatic under the chasuble of the priest for certain liturgical celebrations, such as ordinations.

Cope. A liturgical cape worn by bishops, priests, and deacons for a variety of liturgical celebrations. The cope is worn over alb and stole (and *not* over the dalmatic or chasuble) to provide greater solemnity, and may be used for sacramental celebrations (such as baptisms, weddings, funerals, benedictions) outside of Mass. During Mass, if other sacraments are celebrated, Mass vestments alone suffice.

Humeral Veil. A long, narrow, rectangular vestment. The humeral veil is worn over the shoulders (often over the cope) in order to cover the hands while grasping sacred vessels containing the Body of Christ. For example, the humeral veil is used to hold the monstrance during Benediction of the Blessed Sacrament; it may also be used to hold the monstrance or a ciborium during a Eucharistic procession.

Glossary

Boat. The small container used to hold the incense before it is placed into the thurible by the bishop, deacon, or priest.

Book of the Gospels. The liturgical book that contains the Gospels proclaimed at Mass. The Gospel readings are also contained in the Lectionary, but the Book of the Gospels has a rich history as the particular responsibility of the deacon. For example, the bishop presents the Book of the Gospels to the newly ordained deacon with the charge, "Receive the Gospel of Christ, whose herald you now are: Believe what you read, teach what you believe, and practice what you teach."

Cathedra. The bishop's chair, the sign of his teaching authority. The bishop's church, known as a cathedral, takes its name from this chair.

Chalice. A cup used to hold the wine to be consecrated at the Mass. It is often made from precious metals, although contemporary requirements state only that it must be of a nonporous material of suitable dignity.

Ciborium. A vessel used to hold the hosts used at communion or to store consecrated hosts after Mass. Often very similar in style to the chalice, except that the ciborium (plural: *ciboria*) has a fitted cover.

Collect. The prayer that gathers together ("collects") the prayers of the assembly at the beginning of the Mass. This is the same prayer that is frequently referred to as the Opening Prayer.

Epiclesis. An invocation of the Holy Spirit. In the Eucharistic Prayers of the Latin Church, the Holy Spirit is called upon to bless the gifts of bread and wine (before the words of institution) and to bless the people of God assembled (after the words of institution). An *epiclesis* is found in other sacramental celebrations, such as ordinations.

Gradual. The Responsorial Psalm sung or recited after the first reading from sacred scripture at Mass. The *graduale* is a liturgical book containing these and similar sung texts for the Mass.

Lectionary. The portion of the Roman Missal, published separately, that contains the readings and associated responsorial psalms and acclamations used during the Mass.

Paten. A flat platelike vessel used to hold the host during the Mass. Some patens have a handle extending from it so that it may be held by a server under the chin of a communicant during the distribution of communion. In this case, if a host is dropped during communion, it would fall on the paten and not on the ground.

Roman Missal. The normative text for the Divine Liturgy of the Latin Church. From about the ninth century until the Second Vatican Council, the Roman Missal contained the texts used at Mass, including the readings, chants, and the Order of Mass. As part of the liturgical reforms following the council, the more ancient practice of separate volumes was restored, resulting in the *Sacramentary* and the *Lectionary.*

Sacramentary. The portion of the Roman Missal, published separately, that contains the rubrics, prayers, and other material used by the bishop, priest, and deacon during the Mass.

Thurible (Censer). A vessel for burning incense, usually hung from a chain or chains so that it may be swung freely. It is used quite frequently during the Divine Liturgy of the Eastern Catholic Churches, and during solemn celebrations in the Latin Rite. The thurible is often used by the deacon. The altar server charged with the responsibility for the thurible is called the *thurifer.*

Bibliography

Code of Canon Law: Latin-English Edition. Washington, DC: Canon Law Society of America, 1999.

Congregation for Catholic Education. *Basic Norms for the Formation of Permanent Deacons*. Vatican City: Libreria Editrice Vaticana, 1998.

Congregation for the Clergy. *Directory for the Ministry and Life of Permanent Deacons*. Vatican City: Libreria Editrice Vaticana, 1998.

_____ et al. *Instruction on Certain Questions Regarding the Collaboration of the Non-Ordained Faithful in the Ministry of Priest*. Vatican City: Libreria Editrice Vaticana, 1997.

Cummings, Owen F., William T. Ditewig, and Richard R. Gaillardetz. *Theology of the Diaconate: State of the Question*. New York/Mahwah, NJ: Paulist Press, 2005.

Ditewig, William T. *101 Questions and Answers on Deacons*. New York/Mahwah, NJ: Paulist Press, 2004.

Kasper, Walter. *Leadership in the Church: How Traditional Roles Can Help Serve the Christian Community Today.* New York: Herder and Herder, 2003.

Kwatera, Michael. *The Liturgical Ministry of Deacons.* Second Edition. Collegeville, MN: Liturgical Press, 2005.

Paul VI. *Hodie concilium. AAS* 58 (1966).

Provost, James H., ed. *Official Ministry in a New Age.* Permanent Seminar Studies No. 3. Washington, DC: Canon Law Society of America, 1981.

Smolarski, Dennis C. *How Not to Say Mass,* rev. ed. New York/Mahwah, NJ: Paulist Press, 2003.

Tanner, Norman P., ed. *Decrees of the Ecumenical Councils.* 2 vols. Washington, DC: Georgetown University Press, 1990.

The Documents of Vatican II, All Sixteen Official Texts Promulgated by the Ecumenical Council 1963–65. Walter M. Abbott, ed. New York: Guild Press, 1966.